ON
DEATH,
DYING,
AND
DISBELIEF

ON
DEATH,
DYING,
AND
DISBELIEF

Candace R. M. Gorham, LCMHCS

PITCHSTONE PUBLISHING
DURHAM, NORTH CAROLINA

Pitchstone Publishing
Durham, North Carolina
www.pitchstonebooks.com

10 9 8 7 6 5 4 3 2 1

Library of Congress Cataloging-in-Publication Data

Names: Gorham, Candace R. M., author.
Title: On death, dying, and disbelief / Candace R. M. Gorham, LCMHCS.
Description: Durham, North Carolina : Pitchstone Publishing, [2021] |
    Includes bibliographical references. | Summary: "Offers advice to those
    who are grieving the loss of a loved one but who do not believe in a God
    or afterlife"— Provided by publisher.
Identifiers: LCCN 2021028122 (print) | LCCN 2021028123 (ebook) | ISBN
    9781634312158 (paperback) | ISBN 9781634312165 (ebook)
Subjects: LCSH: Grief. | Death. | Atheism. | Emotions—Psychological
    aspects.
Classification: LCC BF575.G7 G6864 2021 (print) | LCC BF575.G7 (ebook) |
    DDC 155.9/37—dc23
LC record available at https://lccn.loc.gov/2021028122
LC ebook record available at https://lccn.loc.gov/2021028123

To The Boy Who Called Me By My Full Name:
What I wouldn't give to hear you say it one more time.

Contents

Preface

I've always been a heavy griever. My first memory of grieving is leaving my paternal grandfather's funeral when I was six years old. My father was driving our maroon Buick Skylark, crawling slowly along the gravel parking lot of the church and carrying me away from my grandfather, the grandfather who would bounce me on his knee and make me laugh with silly faces. I was sitting on my knees looking out of the back window, sobbing loudly, watching the cemetery get smaller and smaller. My mother was pulling at my dress to get me to turn around; my brother and sister were statues to my left and right. My father told my mother, "Leave her alone. Let her cry." And then she did. She left me there. They all left me there, next to the hot back window, turned around with my arms outstretched on the seat's ridge, sobbing as I came to the realization that Grand-daddy wouldn't be coming back to The House.

I don't remember ever seeing any of my family members grieve—at least not like me. I remember seeing my sister cry briefly once when one of our dogs got hit by a car. I also remember crying so deeply as I watched my father bury that dog in the backyard that my mother made me come in the house. I believe I saw my sister and my mother cry a few times, though I don't recall why and I don't remember ever seeing my father cry. I think I saw my brother cry once, but I'm not sure. The point is, I'm clearly the heaviest griever in my family—at least when measured by affect. I think they would all agree that, in our family, I am the one who openly expresses emotions the most. They would probably also say that I am the most emotional in general—a drama queen, they might even say, but that's a different discussion.

I know, *everyone grieves in their own way*. But this concept doesn't stop us from trying to figure how to grieve. "Everyone grieves in their own way" and "There's no time limit on grief" are the two most common sentiments that people express in an effort to comfort those in mourning. Despite this ubiquitous wisdom, those in mourning rarely find comfort in such assurances. The people expressing these sentiments rarely find much comfort in them either. The advice is vague and does little to alleviate their sense of helplessness. That's why, despite the simplicity of these two concepts, there is a massive industry for helping people who have recently lost someone. One can now swim in a pool of books, workbooks, workshops, self-help groups, support groups, retreats, and psychotherapy, that all tell people how to grieve.

As a mental health professional, I'm in quite a quandary when someone comes to me, personally or professionally, for advice about grieving. While I agree with the premises that everyone grieves in their own way and there is no time limit on grief, I also deeply understand the quest for relief. I never tell anyone how to grieve, but the truth of the matter is that there are things that can make the grieving process better. There are things that are important to pay attention to when in mourning. There are ways in which others can help. The problem is that grief blinds the mourner with dark, heavy clouds of blackness and blankets them in weighted shrouds of nothingness. Sometimes they need others to see for them. Sometimes they need others to feel for them. Sometimes they need others to think for them. Sometimes they just need others. And that is why the grief support industry thrives. What is lacking from that industry, however, is support for grieving nontheists. Nontheists are starved for support of a nonreligious or nonspiritual nature. They are looking for practical advice, just like everyone else, but they also need a special kind of support that makes room for their own particular existential struggle.

I chose to write this book for a number of reasons. First, whenever I attend an atheist or humanist event, people often ask me about grief and mourning. They want to know whether I think it's okay for an atheist to go to a church funeral. They express their confusion at why some nonbelievers turn to god after a loved one dies. They ask for advice on how to support a grieving Christian even though they don't believe in the afterlife. Sometimes I have a response. Sometimes I don't. I would love to have a response to all such questions.

Another reason that I decided to write this book is that, as of this writing, we are in the midst of an enormous, terrifying, deadly pandemic. It has led to hundreds of millions of infections and millions of deaths. I want nontheists to have something to help them as the devastating effects of COVID-19 will ripple for years to come.

And finally, I saw the book as a way to work through my own grief. This is the glue that holds the whole project together and connected me to the writing process. My high school sweetheart died on June 16, 2019, from injuries sustained in a car crash more than two weeks earlier. His name is Tim. I met Tim in the spring of 1996, and my fifteen-year-old heart was crushing immediately. By the time he asked me to be his girlfriend that summer, I was speechless with excitement that he had "chosen" me. (I was young. Forgive me.) By Christmas, when he first told me he loved me, I knew I'd love him for the rest of my life.

I know this experience occurred a long time ago and reflecting through grieving eyes makes things look different, but I truly believe that we had a wonderful relationship. I believe that I was incredibly lucky to have had the kind of relationship that I had at such a young age. We were together two and a half years, but ultimately, differences over religion led to our break up. Then, after I graduated high school, I left my hometown and moved an hour away to college. It broke every piece of my heart—and I would later find out his, too—to leave him behind, and I cried incessantly for months afterward. I knew that, aside from that one issue, there was nothing else that kept us apart. Life moved on, and I met the man who would become my best friend and husband of fourteen years.

I was lucky to have had an amazing marriage with a wonderful man and father to my daughter. However, throughout our marriage, I never stopped wondering about Tim. *How is he? Is he happy? Could we have been happy? Does he think of me? Is he mad at me for moving away? Could we have resolved our differences over religion? Does he still love me? Do I still love him?* Even with those thoughts, overall, my marriage was a happy one. In 2014, my marriage broke up. The reasons are highly personal, complicated, and bizarre, to say the least. But to understand my grief, it is important to know that I have mourned my ex-husband—who is still alive—as if he is dead, and I am not simply being melodramatic.

Coincidentally, Tim's marriage broke up in 2014 too. A mutual friend helped us reconnect, and we became a significant support to each other as we navigated the rough seas of separation and divorce. It was instantly apparent that our love for one another had not waned over the years. And I am not referring to sexual love only, as it would be months before we were physically intimate again. No. We were immediately emotionally intimate. We were able to support each other in the various ways that each of us needed without pressure to be or do anything more. Often when people get out of long-term relationships, they run to others for immediate comfort that quickly turns sexual in nature, which, in turn, can lay a shaky foundation for a relationship.

However, Tim and I did not do that. We rebuilt our friendship and the trust that had been broken many years prior. We took our time getting to know one another again, realizing that the core of what we loved about each other had not changed. There did come a time, however, when we drifted apart again. My father was diagnosed with stage 4 cancer in 2015, and by the end of that year, I was getting invitations for more and more speaking engagements. Then, in spring 2016, my mother had an aneurysm. In addition to caring for my ailing mother and father, navigating issues with my ex-husband still, and engaging in activism, I did not make as much time for Tim as I now wish I had. I cannot blame Tim for making a life for himself in the meantime.

For several years, even though we didn't see or talk to each other on a regular basis, we did periodically make time for each other. The amount of time we spent together varied based on circumstances. For example, in 2017, I was working a job in his city and we saw each other much more regularly. However, in 2018, when I started working in a town that was two hours away from his city, I didn't get to see him nearly as much. Although Tim never remarried, he wasn't immediately available to form a committed relationship with me. As a formerly married man, he valued his freedom.

We talked openly about other people we were seeing. We shared advice on love and admonished each other's stupid mistakes. And above all, we cherished our opportunities to love each other fully without having to hide any parts of ourselves. It was honesty. I could be an unabashed atheist with him, even express antitheist sentiments at times. He admitted that he didn't believe everything in the Bible and wasn't even sure if he could call himself a Christian. We talked about plans for our future and how we could be what the other wanted and needed while remaining true to ourselves. We agreed that we were miserable apart, but we could not figure out how to be together. We clumsily clamored for a way to comfortably be one another's soulmate.*

The night of May 31, 2019, the road was slick with rain, darkened by the grove of crape myrtle trees that line West Market Street. At 8:31 p.m., rounding a curve, Tim, according to the police report, "was exceeding a safe speed for the wet roadway." He was also not wearing a seatbelt. Speeding and not wearing a seatbelt were two things I had nagged him about on multiple occasions. In fact, just a few months prior, I had fussed about it. He said something to the effect of, "Please! You don't care about me." And I distinctly remember saying, "Are you crazy? I'd lose my mind if you died." He followed up with something about not being worried about dying because he had lived his best life: "If it's my time, then, hey, it's my time." And I clearly remember responding, "Well, I need you to live."*

For fourteen days they did all they could at the hospital, but they could not get the swelling in his head down. He was pronounced brain dead on June 14, 2019. The family wanted to allow friends and family the opportunity to say their goodbyes, so they decided to leave him on the machine for a short period of time. I had originally been told that they were going to leave him on the machine until noon on the sixteenth, and I planned to go that morning. The family ultimately decided to take him off the machine early that morning. Once again, I missed my opportunity. If you were to search online, you might find the fourteenth listed as his date of death in the press. It's even on his gravestone. However, the family listed the sixteenth on his obituary, and this is the date they commemorate. When I got a memorial tattoo, I chose to go with this date, June 16. His death was especially devastating to his family because, in 2019, Father's Day was on June 16. Only a week later was Tim's birthday, June 24.

At the funeral, I was overwhelmingly inconsolable. When I say I was inconsolable, it was like something out of a movie. I was rocking back and forth in the pews before the funeral started. I went through several of those absurdly small boxes of tissues. I went outside once to get air and wanted to kneel on the ground. I guess people thought I was fainting because several people rushed over and grabbed me to try to keep me standing, at which point I yelled, "Let me go! Let me go!" and flailed about to shake free of their hands. When I finally did make it to the ground, I beat the pavement, sobbing uncontrollably. Once I finally made it back inside and they were having one last round of viewing before closing the casket, a friend encouraged me to walk by a second and final time. Like a child, I buried my face in her shoulder and cried and resisted. But knowing what was best for me, she placed her arms around me on one side, and another friend held me on the other side, and together they supported me up the aisle. As I got closer, Tim's brother saw me coming and gave me the biggest, most compassionate bear hug that I didn't know I needed. I cried harder.*

Then I saw Tim lying there. He looked nothing like the man I had loved for twenty-three years. When I turned away, his mother was right there. She too opened her arms with a knowing smile and embraced me so lovingly. At that point, I truly felt like I was going to faint in front of the whole church, and I began moving as quickly as I could to the front door without running. My friends who had come with me had to jog to catch up with me. On the steps of the church, I flung myself down, this time sitting, and began sobbing loudly. The friend who had urged me to view him a second time sat beside me, holding me as I was bent over on myself. She pulled me onto her lap and let me cry until I laughed about ruining her dress. Then we made it back into the church just before the doors closed and service started. But oh, was it a terrible funeral experience for me!

For months, the world was nothingness.

I merely floated in it.

Weeks went by before I stopped crying upon waking, and it would be months before I could wake up with any normalcy. I visited the cemetery at least once a week. It may seem creepy, but there was something comforting about going, something tangible. I would sit beside his fresh grave, flowers bright and dirt mound high, sometimes for an hour or more. I would talk to him or fuss at him or just sit in silent tears. Sometimes, I would sit in my car crying, looking at his grave from a distance. And I would repeat this ritual the next week and the next week and the next. For months this went on, and I found that it reduced the intensity of the pain, at first for about twenty-four hours, then for progressively longer periods of time. It was like a drug. Inevitably I always yearned to return to his side.

For months, I existed in smoke and clouds without energy or drive. I couldn't think straight. I didn't socialize. I would lie on the couch with my box of tissues and plastic grocery bag for the trash and let my father and daughter live around me. I barely ate or drank. I actually got very sick and had to go to the doctor for severe dehydration. I even developed mild tachycardia. Luckily everything resolved itself once I began eating and drinking a little more normally again, but it took intentional work.

It starts like a small ball of lead in my stomach, so heavy that it stretches my organs above, pulling at my lungs, making it harder to breathe. The ball of lead becomes a fire that begins to travel upward, setting my sternum and everything beneath it ablaze. Continuing on an upward march, the flames explode out of my shoulders, up my neck, and set my ears, face, and forehead on fire. Tears begin to flow and the silent "ah-ah-ah" is the sound of pain so intense and sharp that the body is unable to perform its natural functions of exhaling or inhaling. My face and eyes feel like they will burst as I can only periodically gasp for air. At the times when I catch myself audibly sobbing, I stuff my mouth with a towel to stifle the noise. If one were to listen closely, one might hear me saying, "No, no, no, no, no," before I fall back into the much more intense, silent cry. Doubled over in pain or in a fetal position, my arms wrap around my waist, squeezing myself tighter and tighter as if I could hug the pain out of myself.

Like I said, I have always been a heavy griever. A public griever. The death of my beloved pushed my coping skills to the very edge of its outer limits. To have lost my dearest all before age forty tore all that I am to shreds, and I feel utterly broken, beyond repair.* I don't believe in soulmates, but everyone who knew us said that Tim and I were soulmates. I don't know. But to watch his body lowered into the ground has certainly left my soul broken.

As my mourning has moved from weeks and months to now years, I've been shocked by how hard his death hit me. As I slowly regained energy—even if only bit by grudging bit—I decided to channel my grief into something positive. One of my tips to nontheists is to do something in honor of the loved one they lost. I thought I'd take my own advice. I know that Tim would not want me to suffer in the way I have since his death, and I know he absolutely would not want me to suffer for any extended period of time. He always told me how proud he was of me for my writing and activism. I think he would be profoundly honored to know that he inspired this book.*

* * *

There are many people to acknowledge and thank for helping me survive the first year of mourning my love's death. Jon kept me engaged in life with his Saturday night Facebook Watch parties. Maureen comforted me with her many condolence cards. My best friend Michelle of over thirty years loved me unconditionally and even soothed my irrational panic attack when I thought she blocked me on Facebook. (I chalk it up to being in the fog of grief.) My sister Pascha put her work on hold and listened to me while I cried on my bathroom floor . . . multiple times. My daughter Naomi waited on me, hand and foot, when migraines, weakness, and despair bound me to my bed. I can't thank and love my tribe enough.

All while I was writing this book, I was constantly thinking about who I could ask to read the draft for feedback. For writers, our content—especially something as significant as an entire book—is like a baby. It's like gestating, laboring, and delivering a child. Handing our drafts to others is scary. Originally, I really wanted to have a black woman help me with my baby, but over and over my thoughts returned to one intellectual: Alix Jules. Beloved by so many for his wit and insight, Alix is intuitive and supportive. Feeling confident that he could provide me with the keen insight of an unbiased reader that I needed, I also trusted that I could hand him my baby and he would neither hurt my baby nor me.

Alix, your life is so full right now. Your beautiful children keep you busy. You have school, an exciting new job, and your own activism to attend to. But the day that I timidly asked if you would take a look at my book, without a moment's hesitation, you responded, "Send it to me." Thank you, Alix, for helping me grieve.

Throughout the book I talk incessantly about hiking. All who know me know that hiking has become a great passion of mine. I owe it all to Darrel Ray. Without him, I would never have sat in the laurel-filled plains aside the glass lake at the feet of the Maroon Bells, never stood atop the world at fourteen thousand feet on the shoulders of giants among giants. I would have never known how wonderfully terribly 12 percent effective oxygen feels when the reward is snow-capped mountains for as far as the eyes can see.

Darrel, if I could wrap up all of the Colorado Rockies and the Smoky Mountains and place them in my chocolate-covered heart, I would mail them to you in a box, tied with silk ribbon and a bow.* I cannot love and thank you enough for igniting my passion for hiking.

ON
DEATH,
DYING,
AND
DISBELIEF

Introduction

As all manner of lifestyles that do not incorporate belief in the supernatural continue to grow, the need for resources that speak to this nontheistic population grows as well. Death and dying are often so tightly intertwined with the spiritual and supernatural that those of us who do not believe in a god can sometimes feel utterly alone when we experience a loss. While religious people can find comfort in each other or a plethora of support materials, nonbelievers have very few sources of support beyond a small—albeit growing—contingent of likeminded brethren. But before we get into that deeper discussion, I need to take a moment to address a few details that will help you understand the book as you proceed.

Why "Nontheist?"

As more and more people identify somewhere on the nonbelieving scale, ranging from *I don't know* to full-blown *I am certain*, more and more terms emerge to represent them. I have grown to like "nontheist" as a broad-spectrum term that carries less baggage than more commonly used words such as "atheist" or "agnostic." And because discussions about death are often virtually inseparable from discussions about the spiritual, I intentionally wanted to use a term with direct spiritual implications—unlike terms such as "secular" or "freethinker," which more generally speak to social and civic issues.

Even as I present the reasoning behind my choice here, I can imagine that there will be many debates about why I chose this word and whether I am using it incorrectly. I do not want anyone to overthink it. I am a Black American woman writing a book based on my personal and professional experiences in the United States, where spiritual beliefs are generally related to god beliefs. Belief in an afterlife, angels, demons, heaven, or hell almost always connect to a belief in a deity or greater power of some kind. For the purposes of this book, therefore, when I use the term nontheist, I am referring to those who eschew all manner of spiritual beliefs and entities.

A Focus on People and Not Things

Grieving is not limited to a process that one goes through after the death of a person. The loss of material things, opportunities, pets, and relationships can all result in a person grieving just like they would if someone had died. Although the advice I offer in this book could be applied to all kinds of situations, I focus specifically on the death of people in my discussions. As noted, my purpose in writing this book is just as much about my own attempt to process a devastating loss as it is about helping others.

Additionally, on top of the collective grief we feel for deaths that have resulted from civil unrest and race-related violence, many of us grieve for the friends, family, and loved ones we have lost during the pandemic. I shudder to think what new violence or plague awaits us in the future. I hope that we won't soon be looking back at this period of time longing for the good old days. But the likely truth is that, at some point, we will encounter years where the death rate is worse than it was in 2020, which is another reason I am choosing to focus on the loss of people as opposed to all other types of losses.[1]

Pronouns

Throughout the book, I use the gender-neutral pronouns they/their/them over the gendered pronouns he/him/his and she/her/hers. I will not take away from the focus of this book to explain why genderless pronouns are not only more inclusive but also a more appropriate and respectful way to communicate. I trust that readers who do not understand will take the time to educate themselves. I look forward to the day when one does not have to preface their books with this sort of statement to forewarn their militant grammarian readers.

Unpleasant versus Negative Emotions

As a mental health clinician, I make a big deal about not calling emotions negative. There are no negative emotions. Emotions exist. They just are. Every person—the vast majority of people—experiences all of them, perhaps not all to the same degree. We may not always even be aware that we are experiencing them, but we do experience them nonetheless. Just because we do not like a particular emotion does not make it negative. It has its purpose. As an analogy, every human has waste-elimination mechanisms in their body. We may not always like these processes or mechanisms either, but that does not make them negative. They have a vital purpose too.

Humans have the tendency to label anything that they do not like as bad, even if that thing is good for them. Anger can be good for you. It is a motivator. It lets you know that something needs to change. Sadness can cause you to slow your body down long enough to let it rest. Irritability can be a sign that your blood sugar is low and you need to eat. You see my point. Just because an emotion is unpleasant does not mean that it has to be a negative influence in your life. You may choose to respond in a negative way or engage in unhelpful behaviors when experiencing unpleasant behaviors, but that is your choice. That is not the choice of the emotions. The emotions just are. Therefore, I refer to emotions as pleasant or unpleasant, and behaviors as helpful or unhelpful.

Practical Tips and Reflections

This book is not just a book of tips but also of reflections on my personal experiences, including questions, comments, and conundrums I have faced professionally. By no means do I offer an exhaustive list of things one could do to ease the burden of grieving. There are entire sections of bookstores and libraries on grief and grieving. The ten tips I offer in this book were selected based on common questions and conversations I have had with nontheists and are things that have helped me personally. In this regard, I combine my personal awareness of issues unique to nontheists with my professional expertise in mental health counseling, and I try to address this deeply personal subject with the tenderness of one who can fully commiserate with the target audience.

While some of this book is reflective and might, at times, sound like my personal diary, the tips contained herein are meant to be as practical as possible. I hope that those in mourning will find concrete actions that they can take immediately upon reading this book, if they so desire. Indeed, in each chapter, I intentionally give advice that one could act on that very day to help alleviate any grief one might be feeling, even if only for a moment. It is not necessary to read the book in the order presented to benefit from it. Each chapter can be read as a stand-alone essay. Although I might at times make reference to something elsewhere in the book, there is nothing that is discussed in one chapter that is essential to learn before moving on to a subsequent chapter. Therefore, you can skip around and read only the chapters that seem most potentially helpful to you or most applicable to your circumstances. But I do hope you choose to read the entire book.

Poetry and Asterisks

At the beginning of each chapter is a poem that I wrote as part of my coping process. I found writing poetry, which can be both pithy and poignant, to be the best and quickest way to get the intense feelings related to grieving out of me. Unless otherwise noted, each poem was written in the weeks or months immediately following Tim's death. This is yet another window into my grief and an addition to Tim's memorial.

As you read, you will encounter asterisks here and there. In fact, you may have noticed some already and may have wondered why they were in the text. As I have shared, this book is a part of my own mourning process. In some places, it feels like a journal. To keep it even more real and raw with myself and you, the reader, I added an asterisk whenever I began to cry when writing. In those instances, I may have been able to keep writing, or I may have had to stop altogether. As I labor in love, I wanted to acknowledge this pain and to mark the places in my writing where I felt it most acutely.

Tip 1

Yes! You can grieve without there being deeper supernatural meaning.

One of Life's Harshest Realities:
Love's greatest teacher is absence;
Death the maestro.

At times I've heard a grieving nontheist say, "I still hear their voice" or "I see them," and they wonder if they are having a spiritual experience. I think it is a sign that the person is in unimaginable pain. Even those who grew up without religion have been exposed to ideas about an afterlife and other spiritual concepts such as demons, angels, apparitions, and more. It is not uncommon for people who believe in an afterlife to also believe that their loved ones can come back and communicate with them. Therefore, it is not unreasonable that you, having encountered that way of thinking much of your life, might manifest those same internalized concepts during your time of extreme vulnerability.

It is okay that you might wish there is an afterlife when you are grieving. You do not need to feel ashamed or silly about having such thoughts either. During this time, you are desperate for any connection to your loved one, and, unfortunately for those nontheists who generally want nothing to do with spirituality, those spiritual concepts seem to be our only possible way to connect with our loved one. Therefore, it makes sense that you wish they were still living somewhere in an afterlife, watching over or even visiting you.

I have a friend who is currently grieving the death of a lover and she and I talk regularly due to our shared understanding of this unique pain. She asked me about my thoughts on the afterlife and whether I wished Tim was in one. I explained that, yes, there had been times I wished he were in a heaven, but I do not dwell on those thoughts because I do not believe in heaven. For me, the thought of an afterlife does not serve a purpose or bring me comfort. It does not make me uncomfortable either. However, for her, it brought her moments of comfort. So, I supported her in her ability and need to simultaneously carry those contradictory beliefs so that she could experience occasional relief, even though she articulated her full belief that there is no heaven. I think she found comfort in knowing that I had had the same experience, which helped normalize her own thoughts, and that I was proof that such a feeling was temporary.

It is also okay for you to "talk to" your loved one, knowing full well that they are not there. If it will make you feel better, tell yourself that doing so is no different than journaling, except you are saying the words out loud. As with journaling, "talking" to a person who is not really there can be a very cleansing experience. Sometimes we just need to do a little bit of "chimney sweeping," a phrase coined in the late nineteenth century by Austrian physician Josef Breuer. Chimney sweeping is analogous to venting, except chimney sweeping involves talking about everything, not just one particular thing. Breuer's more famous colleague, Sigmund Freud, built on this idea, encouraging his patients to talk about anything and everything that had happened since their last session. Today this type of free association serves as a foundational element of most forms of talk therapy.

It can also be helpful to verbalize all of the things you wish you had said or could say to your loved one. You most likely carry a ton of regrets, and there are probably a million things you wish you had or had not said. Although your loved one is gone, there is something healing about getting those words out of your brain and out of your heart. In counseling, some therapists rely on the empty chair technique from Gestalt Theory, in which their client faces a literal empty chair and talks to it as if someone or something is in it. The client may be addressing another person, themselves, or things such as emotions. Sometimes the client may even switch back and forth between the chairs to role play as they work through their problems.

Have you ever had an argument with someone, then later thought of all kinds of comebacks, points, and counterpoints you wish you had unleashed? How did you handle that? Most likely you replayed an alternate version of the conversation over and over in your head a hundred times or called a friend and told them all the things you wish you had said. Then what did you probably say after you vented like that? *Whew! I feel better now.* That's because saying things out loud, even when we cannot say them directly to the target, feels good.

Five Stages of Grief

The five stages of grief were originally described in psychiatrist Elisabeth Kübler-Ross's 1969 book, *On Death and Dying: What the Dying Have to Teach Doctors, Nurses, Clergy and Their Own Families.* Originally written to address those dealing with anticipatory death, that is, for those who were terminally ill or otherwise on the precipice of death, it was also directed to medical professionals and clergy who could expect to work with the dying and their loved ones in the aftermath of the death.

The five stages of grief—denial, anger, bargaining, depression, and acceptance—are well-known today, but they are often misunderstood. The stages themselves can't fully be summed up with a single word, thus we tend to lose the complexity of how the stages actually manifest in the life of a grieving person. The definitions and explanations of these concepts cannot be fully articulated in one section of a short book, thus I will provide only a cursory explanation of them here. People take entire courses on dealing with grief and attend weekend-long continuing education workshops to immerse themselves in these concepts. Professionals spend their careers specializing in grief work and still have to brush up on their understanding of the five stages of grief.

The most cliché explanation of the five stages is that they go in a specific order. In her follow-up book, *On Grief and Grieving: Finding the Meaning of Grief Through the Five Stages of Loss*, Kübler-Ross and cowriter David Kessler sought to address this misunderstanding:

> The five stages—denial, anger, bargaining, depression, and acceptance—are a part of the framework that makes up our learning to live with the one we lost. They are tools to help us frame and identify what we may be feeling. But they are not stops on some linear timeline in grief. Not everyone goes through all of them or goes in a prescribed order.

So, first and foremost, it is important to rid yourself of any notion that you will grieve in an orderly fashion. You may have figured that out already and be bewildered or perturbed by the fact that you are not progressing in some prescribed order. As Kübler-Ross and Kessler note, some people also assume that you must linger in each stage for a certain length of time.

> People often think of the stages as lasting weeks or months. They forget that the stages are responses to feelings that can last for minutes or hours as we flip in and out of one and then another. We do not enter and leave each individual stage in a linear fashion. We may feel one, then another, and back again to the first one.

Worry not. You are doing fine. You are progressing in just the way you are supposed to progress for *you*.

Denial

Denial can be a complex concept that applies in multiple situations. For example, a person who is terminally ill could literally be in denial and refuse to acknowledge—or even treat—the illness. That understanding of denial is obvious. However, denial can also be more symbolic. You might know full well the reality that your loved one is gone but catch yourself repeating, "I can't believe it." Really, you are struggling to process the truth at the depths of your psyche. You may catch yourself repeatedly asking if they really are gone and replaying the story of the loss. This stage might also be described as shock, in some ways. This stage is a stage of paradoxes. You are aware that the person is gone while also being in a state of perpetual disbelief, trying to find ways to make sense of it all.

I could see where spiritual people might insert supernatural beliefs and experiences at this level. For example, they may think they see the person throughout the day. At the time the person normally gets home from work, a person in mourning might say that they heard the door open and close. A person in the denial stage might also dream about their loved one a lot, something people sometimes consider to be a spiritual experience. These are experiences nontheists might attribute to the denial stage. If you find that friends and family are trying to convince you that such experiences are evidence of a spiritual connection, feel free to ignore them. You can embrace your dreams without believing them to be supernatural experiences. As a result, you are free to ascribe whatever meaning to them you find most helpful to your mourning process. Your dreams can mean whatever you want them to mean. This form of "interpreting" your dreams does not have to be spiritual. For example, imagine that your dreams are your mind's way of keeping your loved ones "alive," or use them as inspiration for a work of art or a novel. This type of approach can be an exercise in taking existential control of your experience.

For nontheists, the denial stage may be related to having difficulty with accepting the finality of the loss. The spiritual person has the afterlife to look forward to, whereas the nontheist does not. Death is truly the end. You may linger in or repeatedly circle back to the denial stage more than the spiritual person as a result of your connection to this reality. If you feel that you are in denial for a long time, keep in mind that it may simply be a function of your rationality, which is a good thing. As a result, you need to be patient with yourself. If you recognize that you are in the denial stage, you can resolve the issues related to that stage much faster and with significantly less pain.

Shock, repeated dreams, replaying stories, ruminating, questioning reality—these all provide evidence that one is in the denial stage, which can feel like being frozen in time. The fact that you are "stuck" in one place is actually beneficial, because it would be too overwhelming to face all five stages at once. Explaining that denial can give a person "moments away from [their] pain," Kübler-Ross and Kessler have this to say:

> This first stage of grieving helps us to survive the loss. In this stage, the world becomes meaningless and overwhelming.

Life makes no sense. We are in a state of shock and denial. We go numb. We wonder how we can go on, if we can go on, why we should go on. We try to find a way to simply get through each day. Denial and shock help us to cope and make survival possible. Denial helps us to pace our feelings of grief. There is a grace in denial. It is nature's way of letting in only as much as we can handle.

Anger

Anger is considered to be the most common emotion. We all experience it multiple times a day. I would suggest that we experience many emotions just as much, if not more than anger. However, it is more socially acceptable to express anger than many other emotions; therefore, we express anger while suppressing others. We have become so adroit at suppressing other emotions that we have practically lost the ability to perceive deeper emotions, and it often takes professional support to identify them. Since anger is our most recognizable emotion, it is no surprise that anger often surfaces once we move past denial and we are finally ready to start experiencing feelings.

Grief anger can be directed in multiple directions at once. You can be mad at doctors, yourself, and your deceased loved one all at once, each for very different reasons. Having experienced the numbness of denial, anger reminds you that you are able to feel. Therefore, you should allow yourself to go through this stage without judging yourself for being angry or trying to find meaning in the anger. Sometimes anger is just anger, and that is okay.

Tim's accident involved him hitting a small grove of crepe myrtle trees. For months, I was very angry at crepe myrtle trees. Unfortunately for me, I live in North Carolina, where crepe myrtles are as common as house flies. So, I was angry a lot. I hated the way they had the nerve to release clouds of peddles from their pink and white blossoms in a gentle breeze. I hated the way birds seemed to think they were safe places from which to sing. I hated how strong and sturdy they were. To this day, I do not think I would ever choose to plant a crepe myrtle in my yard.

Spiritual people often find themselves angry at god. It is not unusual for nontheists to also be mad at god in a bizarre way. Of course, as a nontheist, you do not think there is a real supernatural entity toward which you can direct your anger. Instead, you may be feeling anger at the concept of god. You might be angry at the concept of a god that could have saved your loved one, yet didn't. You might be angry at the people who believe that their god could have saved your loved one. *If their god existed, why didn't it save my loved one? How terrible to teach such a thing! If a god does exist, he/she/they/it is cruel and I hate it even without knowing whether or not it is real!* It is understandable that you, as a mourning nontheist, could be angry at a concept that you do not believe in because you are grappling with a trauma that makes about as much sense as the anger itself. You could accept anything if it explained your loss.

As common as anger is, we are also very uncomfortable with it. People are often surprised that a grieving person could be experiencing so much anger during a time that they expect to see angst and depression. As a result, they try to pacify you or get you to move on quickly. This can create resentment and isolation. You must not be influenced by others and deny yourself the opportunity to be angry. Anger is a rational response to death, and you have permission to be angry. Kübler-Ross and Kessler describe anger as "an anchor, giving temporary structure to the nothingness of loss. At first grief feels like being lost at sea: no connection to anything." They further note that it is important that the people around the grieving individual respect their need to fully experience the anger.

> If we ask people to move through their anger too fast, we only alienate them. Whenever we ask people to be different than they are, or to feel something different, we are not accepting them as they are and where they are. Nobody likes to be asked to change and not be accepted as they are. We like it even less in the midst of grief.

Bargaining

Like the other stages, the concept of bargaining makes perfect sense to a grieving person. But also like the others, it can be deceptively complex. After losing a loved one, you will do anything, everything, to have your loved one back, and you will bargain with anyone, everyone, everything, to have them back. However, the bargaining stage is not only about saying, *"I'll do anything."* This stage is also a stage of "What ifs" and "If onlys" and can be marked by guilt.

What if we had found out about the disease sooner?

If only I had been nicer.

What if I had not caused us to leave late?

If only I could say goodbye.

Just like the other stages, bargaining also serves a protective purpose in its own way. As Kübler-Ross and Kessler describe, it can be an "escape from the pain, a distraction from the sad reality of . . . life without [your loved one]." When you bargain, you also play out these alternate realities and desired positive results. *What if we had found out about the disease sooner* might then result in five minutes of fantasizing about just that—finding and treating the disease early, ensuring the loved one's survival, celebrating the survival, enjoying other mundane activities together, etc. However, this fantasy will eventually come to an end and the heavy feelings of loss will return. But there was profound relief in those five minutes.

The ways in which a spiritual person might bargain with god are obvious. Those in mourning might promise to go to church more, stop cursing, or read the entire Bible. Once again, you could be forgiven for experiencing these thoughts as well, having been raised in our culture. These thoughts might be fleeting or they might linger. Remember, bargaining is about finding relief in any way possible. If that means taking five minutes to play out a "what if" scenario that involves god, then so be it. According to Kübler-Ross and Kessler, you need only be aware that this is what is happening and that it is a perfectly normal experience.

Bargaining may fill the gaps that our strong emotions generally dominate, which often keep suffering at a distance. It allows us to believe that we can restore order to the chaos that has taken over.

Depression

Depression is probably the deepest and most overwhelming of all stages. Although the stages allow you to experience grief in unique ways, each feeling more miserable than the last, depression can truly feel like rock bottom. Kübler-Ross and Kessler explain that "grief enters our lives on a deeper level, deeper than we ever imagined" and that "We withdraw from life, left in a fog of intense sadness, wondering, perhaps, if there is any point in going on alone." Although I will discuss this in greater depth in Tip 5, it is important to understand that the depression experienced at this stage is not the same as clinical depression. However, the two often look the same and you could easily be worried about your psychological stability during this time.

Despite how scary the depression stage can be, it is also necessary to embrace it in order to fully heal. It is not something to fix. According to Kübler-Ross and Kessler, depression has a real effect on your physiological functioning and "is a way for nature to keep us protected by shutting down the nervous system so that we can adapt to something we feel we cannot handle." At this stage, they note, everyone is exhausted in every way—the spiritual and nontheistic alike—and it is not unusual for the griever to be in such despair that they have no desire to connect to anyone or anything, including spiritual supports.

As difficult as it is to endure, depression has elements that can be helpful in grief. It slows us down and allows us to take real stock of the loss. It makes us rebuild ourselves from the ground up. It clears the deck for growth. It takes us to a deeper place in our soul that we would not normally explore.

Kübler-Ross and Kessler provide a unique and unexpectedly comforting way of thinking about and managing this stage:

As tough as it is, depression can be dealt with in a paradoxical way. See it as a visitor, perhaps an unwelcome one, but one who is visiting whether you like it or not. Make a place for your guest. Invite your depression to pull up a chair with you in front of the fire, and sit with it, without looking for a way to escape. Allow the sadness and emptiness to cleanse you and help you explore your loss in its entirety. When you allow yourself to experience depression, it will leave as soon as it has served its purpose in your loss. As you grow stronger, it may return from time to time, but that is how grief works.

Acceptance

Similar to the other stages, the acceptance stage is a process. The common misconception about this stage is that it is the end point. You do not *get to* acceptance. You progress through it. Because people often misunderstand acceptance as an end point, they also mistake it to mean that you have to be okay with the loss. That is not the case. Acceptance is not about being okay with the loss. It is about allowing the loss to be a part of your life in a different way. The acceptance stage is a time of reorganizing life, relationships with others, relationships with the deceased loved one, routines, even the stories you tell yourself about the loss. According to Kübler-Ross and Kessler, "Healing looks like remembering, recollecting, and reorganizing . . . we may become aware of the commonsense reasons for our loss, even if we never actually understand the reasons."

Reorganizing, they note, is about the process of trying to "live in a world where our loved one is missing." It takes time to adjust to no longer getting that morning phone call or not having dinner together every evening. It takes time before you can begin considering who else will take you shopping for a prom dress or walk you down the aisle. It takes times to believe that you can love again.*

As Kübler-Ross and Kessler conclude, it is in the acceptance stage that you are likely to experience the least angst about spiritual concerns.

> Finding acceptance may be just having more good days than bad. As we begin to live again and enjoy our life, we often feel that in doing so, we are betraying our loved one. We can never replace what has been lost, but we can make new connections, new meaningful relationships, new interdependencies. Instead of denying our feelings, we listen to our needs; we move, we change, we grow, we evolve. We may start to reach out to others and become involved in their lives. We invest in our friendships and in our relationship with ourself. We begin to live again, but we cannot do so until we have given grief its time.

You will experience every emotion on the spectrum. You will go through all the stages. You will contemplate and ruminate. You will fantasize and romanticize. And having grown up in a society that places high value on supernatural experiences and entities, the afterlife, and spiritual exploration, it is reasonable that you will find yourself thinking about these things as well. Your friends and family may try to convince you that such thoughts are proof that god is trying to reveal himself to you and you may even wonder about this yourself from time to time. However, whether you are a lifelong nontheist or came to your nontheism after years of study and struggle, you may be uncomfortable with having supernatural thoughts or "experiences" during the grieving process. In those moments, it's important to recognize that such unwanted thoughts are often simply an expression of the grieving process.

Tip 2
Be patient with your spiritual loved ones.

"I'm here if you need me," they say.
But if only they knew how heavy, how ugly things get,
they wouldn't be so quick to offer.
How quickly they trot out the old favorites:
"Things will get better."
"You've got to snap out of it."
They don't understand.
I've been stretched so far.
My elasticity is gone.

One of the five stages of grief is anger. Although that anger might be temporarily directed at anything, the stage is not particularly about becoming an angry person in general. Even though I just encouraged you to embrace your anger in the preceding tip, here I am going to encourage you to be careful about the ways you spend that energy. Tip 2 is about being patient with others who are spiritual so that you do not weigh yourself down with unnecessary unpleasant emotions and experiences.

Unless you are surrounded by nontheists, you will most likely have to deal with some spiritual people during this time of mourning. One thing about death that I find the most frustrating is attending Christian funerals. It can be hard to listen to a minister preach about the deceased being on their way to heaven when everyone knew they were not living a "good Christian life," or worse, if I knew that they were not a Christian at all. As a nontheist, I quickly grow tired of listening to preaching about heaven and angels and how we will all be with Jesus in the sweet by and by. It especially gets under my skin when those conducting the service say that god took the person for a reason, that god had a higher purpose that has not been revealed to us. I get angry when a preacher says that a sick person got their final healing or a baby got their wings. I think, *Why didn't god just stop them from getting sick in the first place?! Nobody wants to hear about a higher purpose! Stop telling these people all these lies!*

What we nontheists have to remember is that the funeral is comforting to those who are spiritual. The funeral is a ritual for the living. If you take the spiritual messages out of it, many of the things I discuss in my tips are taking place during a funeral. People are psychologically and emotionally supporting one another during a ritual designed to honor the dead. People reconnect with nature when they place the body in the ground and cover it with flowers and are afforded a space to cry and cry and cry as much as they want. Their physical bodies are taken care of with food and drink provided afterward. Many people leave funerals feeling cleansed and uplifted.

If your deceased loved one was a nontheist and their friends and family did not know this, now is not the time to "out" them. You might feel the strong desire to set the record straight so that people can truly respect your deceased loved one or honor them correctly. However, the truth is that the only person who would feel better is you, and that is not even guaranteed. If your loved one was not ready to tell their family about their nontheist status, it is not your place to do so, at least not right now. Let the family go on believing whatever they believe. Do not interrupt their grieving process, just as you would not want them to interrupt yours.

Often, we yearn to get to know our loved one better and secrets have a way of revealing themselves in the aftermath of someone's death. Unfortunately, not all of those secrets are pleasant and some people end up hurt even further, with more questions and regrets. Like the proverbial stash of porn magazines hidden in the garage, some secrets are better kept for the emotional health and healing of the living. Over time, some of the family may be open to learning about certain parts of your loved one's life that had been hidden, but do tread lightly. Consider how well you know the people to whom you are talking and the quality of the relationships between them and the deceased. You want to honor your loved one, but you also want to protect the living from unnecessary pain. Ask yourself, *Why am I revealing this information?* Is it out of spite? Is it because doing so would make you feel better? Is it because your loved one was ready to tell the family but never got the chance? Is it because one of your loved one's close friends or relatives wants to know more about them and you believe this is a way for the friend or relative to feel closer to them?

Another scenario that might be particularly enraging is if your deceased loved one was a nontheist and their friends and family knew but are still talking about them as if they were a believer. My ex-husband was an atheist and his family knew it. However, when he became ill, they were all too happy to push him toward religion and take advantage of his failing memory. Try to resist the urge to interrupt the grieving process of the friends and family who say such things. Remember, they are looking for any way to hold on to their loved one, too. They are praying that their loved one is looking down on them from heaven or visiting them at night. They are hoping that their loved one has turned into a guardian angel who will protect them from now on. When they are talking about your loved one in spiritual terms, these may be the times that you have to excuse yourself from social events.

Depending on your relationship with their friends and family, maybe you could gently remind them of your loved one's beliefs and nonbeliefs, but do not let such a reminder turn into a fight. The point is be very careful. Everyone is trying very hard to hold themselves together, and some do a better job at it than others. You never know what is holding someone's sanity in place.

A major issue that often comes up is when spiritual people

try to comfort you. One school of thought is that you should reject offers of spiritual comfort and assert your nontheistic beliefs so that people will stop trying to comfort you in that way. Within that school of thought are two branches. One branch says that you should assert yourself so that you are letting people know what kind of comfort you want and need. It is a form of asking for what you need by telling people what you do not want or need. The other branch says that you should assert yourself so that you remain true to who you are—otherwise you are being a phony.

Another school of thought is to accept a person's comfort without saying anything. I am the sort of person who leans toward accepting a person's comfort if it is coming from a good place. For example, when someone says "bless you" after I sneeze, I usually don't say anything other than "excuse me." That way I am not completely silent after the person said something, and it gives the sense that the reason I didn't say "thank you" was because I was too busy saying "excuse me." In truth, "excuse me" is my immediate and natural response. Luckily, I've been able to drop the "thank you" without much notice. However, I know people who will respond to a "bless you" with something like, "Oh, I don't believe in god. So, you can keep your 'bless yous.'" When people tell me this is how they respond, I always laugh and say, "But we live in America. 'Bless you' is a cultural thing people say. I bet most people say it without even realizing they are saying it."

My daughter is an atheist. One day she said "bless you" to me. When I asked her about it, she paused, thought about it, and acknowledged that she says it without even realizing it and thinks it must just be something she picked up from friends. As a newfangled teenage atheist, she has many Christian friends who neither have a problem with her atheism nor find it remarkable that she says "bless you."

Many of my friends know that I am an atheist. But when Tim died, classic spiritual words of comfort slipped out before they could stop themselves. "You know he's looking down on you." "I'll be praying for you." "The lord is going to help you get through this." Sometimes they would be kind enough to catch themselves and say, "I know you don't believe this stuff, but still." They are my friends. They love me. They loved Tim. Their words came from a good place. Therefore, I graciously accept their comfort. I am too distraught, too broken, too devastated to stop my sobbing soul to fuss at them about my nonbelief.* When you have a burning ball of lead setting you on fire, it is okay to accept any hugs, kisses, and gentle displays of kind affection that can help lighten the burden.

Also remember, people are giving you the only things they have. As inevitable as death is, many people have not experienced a profoundly intense loss such as the loss of a child, close parent, or lover. Therefore, they have absolutely no idea how to comfort others. When I was first told that the doctors were going to perform surgery to try to relieve pressure on Tim's brain, I remember exactly where I was. I was in the office kitchen leaning on a counter, texting with a member of Tim's family. When he told me, I nearly fainted and caught myself with the counter. There was only one coworker in the facility with me, and he happened to be standing near me as I was relaying this new information to him. He managed to hold me before I collapsed further. As he rubbed my back, all he could say was, "I don't know what to say. I'm no good at these things. I'm not good with emotions. It's going to be okay. I wish I knew what to say. Damn. I'm no good at this. It's going to be okay, Candace."*

He was utterly lost. He knew I was an atheist. I bet that if he didn't know that, he probably would have said something about prayer and healing and god. When someone hugs you and tells you that Jesus is going to comfort you and that they will be praying for you, they most likely have no other words because they grew up in a community where those were the only words they heard or were taught.

Being patient with others and not wasting your short supply of energy on misplaced anger does not mean you should let people disrespect you. If the *kind* words are coming from a friend or family member who is well acquainted with your nontheism and they are clearly trying to take advantage of your vulnerability by offering you spiritual words, that would be the time to assert yourself. While you do not want to expend energy on unnecessary arguments, you should not allow being harassed. If someone is telling you that now is the time to repent, is suggesting that the only way you will see your loved one is if you get saved, or keeps trying to have sit-down hold-hands kinds of prayers with you, that might be the time for you to firmly remind them of your atheism and let them know that you would like them to stop their actions.

Tip 3
Take care of your physical self. (Take care of you.)

He would want us to keep living our lives,
assuming his absence left no more than a hole.
He didn't realize that his death
was like an atom bomb going off,
leaving years of devastation and everlasting scars.

As basic as it sounds, *taking care of one's physical self* is easier said than done for the mourner in the depths of grief. When you are at your saddest is when you are at greatest risk of totally neglecting yourself. You must be mindful of attending to your basic needs. A few months before Tim's death, I began dealing with pretty significant unexplained health problems. Being in mourning only made things worse. I stopped eating and drinking. I rapidly lost weight and looked visibly ill. I became dehydrated and developed conditions that needed treatment as a result of it. My existing problems were complicated further because I failed to attend to my most basic needs. Although this chapter may contain a lot of information that seems rudimentary or repetitive, when we are deeply grieved, it is easy to forget the basics. In my deepest despair after Tim's death, it was not that I did not care about my health; it is that I forgot about my health. Sometimes, I needed someone to be my substitute brain because not even my autopilot was working properly.

Drink Water. Eat Food. Drink More Water.

You must remember to eat and drink on a daily basis. If you are having a hard time eating, you must at least drink liquids and stay hydrated. Becoming dehydrated can lead to urinary tract infections, kidney infections, heart problems, and more. Although you might strive to take in the recommended number of ounces of liquid per day, getting in as much as you can is better than nothing. The same is true for food. If you are struggling with your food intake, go for simple foods that are easy on the stomach. Comfort foods such as soup, bread, and crackers would all be good options. These foods provide calories but are also easily tolerated for someone who may be feeling in such despair that they don't want to eat at all. But for those times that you just cannot bring yourself to eat, you must stay hydrated. Drink more liquids—preferably water or noncarbonated, noncaffeinated beverages that will restore electrolytes and provide nutrients. I talk more about food in my discussion on caring for others in Tip 10.

Get Sleep

Lack of sleep can lead to a variety of complications ranging from something as simple as trouble concentrating to extreme conditions such as psychosis. When in mourning, you are already mentally and emotionally compromised. Lack of sleep or a poor sleep routine will exacerbate those problems exponentially. Therefore, a grieving person must remember to get a healthy amount of sleep on a nightly basis. The recommended amount of sleep varies by age group, but eight hours seems to be the average target. In addition to getting the right amount of sleep, there are other aspects of good sleep hygiene that improve health.

As a mental health professional, I place tremendous importance on sleep. My clients will tell you that I harp on sleep all the time and inquire about it during every session. This includes what's generally referred to as sleep hygiene, the practices and routines we follow that allow for good sleep at night and alertness during the day. Some people like myself are lucky enough to be able to fall asleep quickly and sleep soundly most of the night most of the time. For some people, however, they need a true evening routine that helps their body slowly prepare for sleep. That routine might include taking a hot shower, followed by a warm cup of tea, and a book. For too many of us, our evening routine is to watch TV until we are ready to go to bed, and then we get on our smartphones once in bed. We end up spending another hour or more on social media before finally turning the lights off and putting away the phone.

Then a notification goes off that we cannot resist checking and that results in another thirty minutes on the phone. This is not healthy sleep hygiene.

Healthy, sleep-promoting activities that you could put into your evening routine include relaxing activities such as bathing, light stretching, meditating, enjoying warm drinks, listening to calming music, and reading. The key, however, is to turn off the electronics and disengage from any unpleasant or stress-producing activities early enough that this routine has time to works its magic. It is generally recommended that you turn off electronic devices anywhere from thirty to sixty minutes before bed. If you are the type of person who has a hard time winding down, you might need an hour and a half or more.

Turning off your electronic devices, including unnecessary lights and lamps in the home, is a very important item in your sleep hygiene toolkit not to be overlooked. Screens lead to increased exposure to blue light wavelengths. Blue light is beneficial during the daytime as it boosts attention, mood, and reaction time. However, that is not what you need when you are trying to go to sleep. Some newer cell phones give you the option to adjust your light settings in the evening so that you can filter the blue light in the display. Even so, the common advice is to turn off electronic devices thirty to sixty minutes before bed. Some experts take an even tougher stance and recommend turning off electronic screens two to three hours before bed! Can you imagine asking people in the twenty-first century to turn off all electronic devices two to three hours before bed?! But when you are in mourning and not sleeping, you may need to engage in countermeasures that are as radical as your pain.

Another aspect of sleep hygiene to consider is napping. A grieving person can be very tired from crying, entertaining visitors, and planning funerals and memorials. Also, variations in healthy brain chemicals such as dopamine and serotonin that play roles in energy levels can create feelings of sluggishness and exhaustion throughout the day. And while it is understandable that you will go through a period of time where you likely need more sleep than usual, be mindful of your overall functioning and mood. If you find that you cannot sleep at night but are napping throughout the day, it is time to stop napping. All sleep is not created equal. Our bodies have evolved to sleep when the sun goes down. We know this because our brains produce melatonin when the sun goes down and melatonin makes us sleepy. That is why you should limit your daytime naps to no more than one twenty- to thirty-minute nap per day. Use a timer or alarm if necessary, but do not sleep too often or too long during the day.

It is also important to avoid stimulants close to bedtime. Caffeine is the most obvious culprit. Coffee and sodas are the favored boogeymen. However, tobacco also has a stimulating effect and should be avoided close to bedtime as well. People who use tobacco sometimes increase their use while in mourning. People who had previously quit might pick up the habit again, and some might start using for the first time. Long-term detrimental health effects aside, if you are a smoker and find yourself feeling more stimulated, antsy, or keyed up at night, you might want to consider cutting off your tobacco use earlier in the evening. The same is true for alcohol. Although it makes us sleepy, in truth, evening alcohol use leads to poor sleep throughout the night.

People often talk about the impact of nighttime eating on sleep. Anything that triggers indigestion for you should be avoided. It is never a good idea to eat immediately before going to sleep. In fact, I suggest that you stop eating several hours before bed. If you find that you need a snack, make sure it is something that is light and healthy. Examples of foods that are often problematic include rich foods, fatty or fried meals, and spicy dishes. Citrus fruits or highly acidic foods can also trigger heartburn.

Exposure to natural light during the daytime is important as well. While sitting by a window might provide enough light exposure for some, if you find you are having trouble sleeping, you might want to spend time outside each day. When we are grieving, sometimes our nights and days begin to run together, especially during our bereavement days when we are off work and people expect us to be home. This is also true for weekends and holidays, and for those who work from home or work nightshifts. It is easy to look up and realize that several days have gone by and you have not been outside once, not even to get the mail. I work from home and it happens to me all the time. Exposure to natural light during the daytime assists with keeping our circadian rhythm on track, thereby facilitating a healthy sleep-wake cycle.

One final point about healthy sleep hygiene is to consider

your actual sleep environment. When we are grieving, it is easy for us to "pass out" wherever our tired bodies are at the moment. We might nod off on the couch in front of the TV or cry ourselves to sleep on the bathroom floor. However, your sleep environment should be comfortable and comforting. Obviously having a supportive mattress is important, but they are expensive. If you have an uncomfortable mattress and cannot afford a new one, you might consider getting a mattress topper. Also, a new pillow or set of linens might be just what you need. Sleep professionals recommend that the temperature of the bedroom be between 60 and 67 degrees. Too hot or too cold and you'll find yourself tossing and turning.

At night, consider blackout curtains, eyeshades, earplugs, and white noise machines to eliminate distracting sounds and lights. Turn off lamps, night lights, and even bedside clocks that emit light or sound. Turn your phone off or at least turn off extraneous alerts—texts, social media, games, reminders, etc.—so that the only thing that comes through are phone calls and wake alarms. You could even go so far as to put your phone in "Do Not Disturb" mode and allow only people in your emergency contacts to get through via a phone call. Also think about smells. Try using lavender fabric softener, room mist, or plug-in air fresheners (not the kind with lights!) to add an additional layer of comfort to your room. The more you please, or disengage altogether, each of your senses, the better.

Take Your Medicine

Whether for medical conditions, mental health needs, or supplementary purposes, continuing to take your medications daily is absolutely essential. Everything in this chapter is essential, but failing to take your medication can become a life or death problem rather quickly. Immediately after Tim's death, I remember making a Facebook post:

> Drink water. Take meds. Get sleep. Repeat.
> I will do that for him.
> Drink water. Take meds. Get sleep. Repeat.

As a person who takes medications for both medical conditions and mental health needs, I know that even one week without either of these medications and I begin to have significant side effects. By two weeks, I will be in withdrawal, feeling sick and struggling to function. One thing that I found I struggled with was keeping up with the refills. Going to the pharmacy every thirty days became such a taxing chore. As a result, there were times I ran out of one medication or another, though typically only for a day or two. Eventually I was lucky enough to have the opportunity to switch to a mail-order pharmacy that ships three months of medications at a time. I am being only slightly hyperbolic when I say it has literally been a lifesaver.

If you find that keeping up with your prescriptions is difficult, consider using a mail-order pharmacy. If that is not an option, more and more pharmacies are beginning to offer delivery services. You should also look into switching to ninety-day supplies, if it is affordable or your insurance will pay for it. In fact, there are a lot of medications that are actually cheaper when you buy them three months at a time. If you have a hard time remembering whether or not you took your medications, buy a pill organizer. You can get these from the pharmacy for a few dollars and they range in size. You can get a simple Sunday-through-Saturday organizer that has one well per day or you can get more elaborate ones that have "Breakfast," "Lunch," and "Dinner" wells, or wells with actual times of day written on them. The pill boxes also come in a variety of sizes to accommodate large pills or large quantities of pills.

Develop a routine for actually taking the medications. For example, I have all of my morning meds in a drawer beside the refrigerator. When I go downstairs in the morning, I immediately head to the pill drawer and get that part of my day out of the way. My evening meds are on my nightstand beside my bed. I tend to take those either just before I turn out the light or when I am close to going to sleep. I don't use a pill box consistently, but when I am going through a stressful time in my life and find that I keep forgetting to take my medications or cannot remember whether I took them, I will start using the pill box.

See Your Doctor

Part of taking care of yourself is also about going to the doctor when you need to. Keep scheduled appointments. Do not reschedule them, no matter how bad you feel. In fact, keep the appointments and tell your doctor about your loss. Your grief might be contributing to your problems, if you are, in fact, going to the doctor because of a problem. If you are going to the doctor as part of routine care, it is still important to keep that appointment and to tell your doctor about your loss. If it is routine care, that suggests you have a lasting relationship with the doctor and they would probably like to be kept abreast of significant changes in your life.

Keeping your appointments with your doctor is also important to ensure that you have sufficient refills on record at the pharmacy. It is quite a headache to run out of refills then have to wait on the pharmacy and doctor's office to do their little back and forth, which might take days. Go to your doctor's appointments. Ensure there are refills on file at the pharmacy. Save yourself a headache.

It is also important to go to the doctor and not just assume that your issues are merely a result of being in mourning. As I said before, I became very ill while in the darkest parts of my grief. I became so ill that there was no way for me to avoid going to the doctor. However, had I gone sooner, things would not have gotten as bad as they did. Instead, I let my despair hold me back from going and I paid a very painful price for it.

Exercise

No discussion of self-care would be complete without talking about exercise. When you are grieving, you barely have enough energy to blink. For some people, they naturally gravitate toward hard workouts to manage stress, but many of us do just the opposite when stressed and depressed. We cocoon and become less active. For many grieving people, being asked to exercise is like being asked to take a deep breath under water. It ain't gonna happen. But if you can just get your head above water a little bit, you can breathe. And if you can just move your body a little bit, you can exercise. Exercise does not have to be a strenuous hour-long gym session.

So often I hear people—usually men (sorry, men)—say, *Nah. I like to go hard! If I'm going to work out, I'm going to work out hard!* They go to the gym for two-hour sessions, five days a week for two weeks then that is it. They pull a muscle or get too busy or just plain realize how hard *go hard* is, and they flame out before they really got going. That is not what you want to do when you are grieving.

Several years ago, I lost 130 pounds (intentionally in this instance). The way I started was that, in addition to dietary changes, I took twenty-minute walks or rides on the elliptical machine three days per week. That was it. I kept it light and easy for a reason. I did not want to psychologically burn myself out. I wanted to be able to say to myself, *This is easy. I can do this.* And slowly, I added more time and began running. That is how you should approach exercise during times of grief. Do not push yourself too hard. The goal is to get moving, not to *go hard or go home.* The exercise is going to be good for your physical health as well as your mental and emotional health. It also has the added benefit of helping you sleep at night. Whether walking on a treadmill in the house or taking a walk around the block, going to the gym or a yoga studio, any amount of activity that gets your body moving and stretching and your blood pumping is going to be beneficial.

Medical recommendations for exercise are usually in the range of thirty minutes per day, three days per week. Today, with so many people using smart watches that count steps, a common recommendation is 10,000 steps per day. Taking that many steps each day is harder than you might think, especially if you work a desk job or live in an area where people mostly drive to get around. If you are hitting 10,000 steps per day, you are being fairly active as it is. But for those of us who can't seem to reach 10,000 steps per day on a regular basis, twenty to thirty minutes of walking three days per week is a good place to start.

Attend to Your Hygiene

When you are grieving, the days begin to run together and the line that marks day and night gets blurry, especially if you are not leaving the house much. As a result, it is easy for several days to go by without taking a shower, changing clothes, or even brushing your teeth. When you are deeply grieving, you may be questioning whether or not you even want to keep living at all. Being fresh and clean does not even register as a concern when you are mentally and emotionally in that kind of space. However, a hot shower or warm bath can go a long way toward lifting your mood and washing away the mental fog that you find yourself stuck in.

Consider the timing of your shower or bath. A bath is good to take at night when you need to relax for bed. A shower might be good in the morning when you need to wake up.

Most people have a preference for bathing either in the morning or at night. However, you may need to be more intentional about your bathing routine based on your needs. For example, I prefer to shower at night. However, I had a much harder time getting up and getting my day going than I did falling asleep at night. I realized that a morning shower with refreshing shower gels or soaps helped energize me for my day. So, for quite a while I switched to taking showers in the morning. Of course, I could have still taken a shower at night if I was really dedicated to nighttime showering. However, the problem was that I would sometimes go several days without bathing at all. The morning showers were my best bet for ensuring that I bathed regularly and for helping to get my days off to a better start.

Although you can get away without bathing daily, you should definitely attend to your oral hygiene daily. Of course, dentists recommend that you brush your teeth after each meal. Many people strive to brush their teeth every morning and at night before bed. When in mourning, you may fail to brush your teeth for days at a time altogether. However, for your health and comfort, I recommend that you at least brush your teeth every morning. In the morning, go straight to the bathroom and brush your teeth immediately. If you have to brush your teeth while crying, so be it. I've done it, too.

Clean clothes are just as much a part of your hygiene as bathing and brushing your teeth. It is easy to wear the same outfit every day for a week, especially if you aren't bathing daily. But even if you are bathing daily, you still might be tempted to keep putting on the same oversized sweatpants and hoodie.

While many people wear the same pajamas several nights before finally throwing them into the dirty clothes hamper, you
do not want to wear soiled or smelly clothes for days. If you are
wearing the same clothes all day and night, you need to force
yourself to swap them out. Putting on a fresh outfit or pajamas,
especially after bathing, will do wonders in regard to making
you feel lighter and more peaceful.

In addition to your clothes, do not forget about your bed
linens and bathroom towels. Washing these and changing
them out for cleans ones will also make a difference in how
you feel. A fresh towel for drying can help you feel cleaner and
pleasantly scented sheets will facilitate better sleep.

Substance Use and Abuse

I could have chosen to talk about substance use and abuse in
the chapter on mental health, but I have chosen to include it
in this chapter for a specific reason. When grieving, we will do
anything to feel better. I do not want to pathologize attempts
to feel better. Of course, disruptive behaviors that go too far or
last too long can become pathological. However, it is not uncommon to see people increase or start using alcohol and other
drugs during times of grief.

Cheap, accessible, and legal for those of age, alcohol is the
most socially acceptable drug to use and the most commonly
used one. As a depressant to the central nervous system, alcohol offers solace by numbing the mind and body. It brings
relaxation and sleep where there may not have been any. It low-
ers inhibitions and allows for cathartic crying. It frees the mind

from obsessive thoughts and gives the griever opportunities to socialize and laugh. Unfortunately, the truth is that alcohol has a number of negative effects on the body that can eventually worsen the mental and emotional exhaustion we are trying to overcome at the very time that we need our total health the most. While we might initially fall asleep quickly with alcohol, ultimately it is not good for sleep and leads to worse sleep quality overall. Further, alcohol dehydrates the body and is full of simple carbohydrates that are not good for your health. Binge drinking can lead to psychosis and worse, death.

A simple screening that mental health professionals use to assess for problematic alcohol use is called the CAGE questionnaire.

*Have you ever felt you needed to **Cut down** on your drinking?*

*Have people **Annoyed** you by criticizing your drinking?*

*Have you ever felt **Guilty** about drinking?*

*Have you ever felt you needed a drink first thing in the morning (**Eye-opener**) to steady your nerves or to get rid of a hangover?*

If you answer *no* to all questions or *yes* to only one of them, the screening is considered to be negative. If you answer *yes* to two or more, the screening is considered to be positive. The CAGE questionnaire does not diagnose alcoholism. It has been found to be highly correlated with drinking patterns that rise to the level of diagnosable disorders. Therefore, the more items to which you respond in the affirmative, the more you should honestly reflect on your alcohol consumption.

Prescription medications are also often abused and grievers need to be mindful of their prescription drug use. First and foremost, it is very important that we only take medication that is prescribed to us. In the next chapter I discuss the benefits of psychotropic medications, but I'll mention anti-anxiety medications here briefly as they are easy to obtain and highly addicting. Anti-anxiety medications can provide great relief during these times. Not surprisingly, they are easy to buy on the street. It is important to resist the urge to buy Xanax (alprazolam), Ativan (lorazepam), Klonipin (clonazepam), and other similar medications off of the streets and to get these medications from a physician or psychiatrist when necessary. These are powerful drugs and have significant negative drug interactions with many other medications if not taken carefully.

Other prescription drugs, particularly painkillers such as opioids, have caused such a problem in our society that opioid abuse has been deemed a national public health emergency. Just like with anti-anxiety medications, painkillers such as OxyContin (oxycodone) and Percocet are highly effective at helping us relax. They are also highly addicting and the human body quickly becomes physically dependent on these medications. Physical dependence is what makes stopping the use of these drugs particularly difficult in comparison to other drugs. Physical dependence is what leads to withdrawals. Opioid withdrawal can be very dangerous and sometimes requires medical assistance. It may be surprising to some to learn that, in truth, alcohol withdrawal is actually among the most dangerous of them all, and severe alcoholics definitely need medical intervention to ensure they do not get sick, or even die, during severe alcohol withdrawal.

In regard to marijuana, the research is becoming more and more clear with every passing year that marijuana has many medicinal applications. More than half of U.S. states now allow medical marijuana, and the number of states that allow legal recreational use grows annually as well. I am an advocate of full marijuana legalization and support its use to manage a multitude of mental, emotional, and physical health issues. Due to the fact that excessive consumption of anything, even water, can have deleterious effects, I do recommend that individuals consult with their doctors first to discuss its use, contraindications, and other such concerns. I also am not suggesting that anyone violate any state or federal laws.

While grieving, two things happen: you stop caring and you become forgetful. That's why so much of taking care of yourself is about establishing good routines and strategies to stay on top of things. You may have to mix up your usual routine because it no longer fits in your day. Perhaps part of your day was structured in a certain way based on your deceased loved one being there. Now that they are no longer there, your old structure no longer works. Some of your preferences may not be feasible right now because you really prefer to do nothing. You need to try something new. Perhaps your once impeccable memory now seems like a garbage can. You may need to utilize tools such as sticky notes or phone reminders. I have been known to write on my bathroom mirror with a dry erase marker.

While in the deepest parts of your grief, the key to taking care of your physical health is to put as many things as possible on autopilot by developing routines and using tools to facilitate those routines. Eventually you will have to take over the reins in order to keep living, but for that period of time when you are not even sure if you want to keep living, the autopilot is good. If your autopilot does not work, you will need to depend on other people to be your brain. That is why books like this with tips are beneficial and friends and family who will help you complete basic tasks or manage your day-to-day routines are priceless. You know that your loved one would want you to continue living and loving your life. Taking care of your physical body is just another way to honor your loved one.

Tip 4
Attend to your psychological and emotional needs.

The devastation is profound.
It is complete.
Marked by jagged edges below steep, rocky cliffs.
I'm less secure,
Uncertain.
It has worn away at my mind.
The recovery is painful.
Incomplete.
Impossible.
Without your voice,
Unheard in so long,
Recovery was a facade.

Dealing with the loss of a loved one will burn you out in many ways, not least of which is psychological and emotional. Unfortunately, while many people recognize that experiencing mood swings is a normal part of grieving, often they do not think they can do anything about them. People usually fall into one of two camps when it comes to addressing psychological and emotional concerns during times of mourning. People in Camp A believe that you do not need to do anything. You should just let yourself feel as many feelings as you want to feel and let them resolve on their own. People in Camp B believe that you should try to contain your emotions. Otherwise, they could get out of control, consume you, and destroy your life. If you fall into one of these two camps, I suggest you consider an approach that incorporates elements from both of these phi-losophies: you should let yourself feel as many feelings as you want to feel but recognize that there are actions that you can— and should—take to make yourself resilient, thereby prevent-ing the emotions from consuming and destroying your life.

See a Therapist

As a licensed mental health professional, I do not think I could even talk about dealing with grief without imploring you to consider seeing a therapist. The mental health professional was once believed to work only with the very sick, people with severe and persistent illnesses like schizophrenia and bipolar disorders. But that simply is not the case. Mental health pro-fessionals work with people along the full spectrum from *the worried well* to those who likely will never get out of an institu-tion, from children in schools to individuals in rehab. Mental health support is for everyone and I suggest that you consider it for yourself.

Grieving is an extremely lonely process. Besides those times when I have experienced clinical depression episodes, I have never felt more alone than when I am feeling extremely grieved. Either it feels like no one understands or I worry that people are tired of me talking about my loss. These are very common sentiments. Every person I know who has ever suffered a profound loss has told me that they had those same persistent thoughts and worries. Regardless of how many people claim to be there for us, we just cannot seem to shake the feeling that they are not telling us the truth. They do not mean it. They do not want to be here for us. They do not know what they are getting themselves into. They could not handle the heaviness of this despair. And so, we just keep it to ourselves.

A therapist is trained to be and do exactly the opposite of all of those things. They have the professional skills to sit with the heaviest pains and support people as they struggle through the morass of despair that is the grieving process. Therapists are trained to do this day after day without giving up on their clients. To be sure, therapists have to do their own self-care, but that is not the client's concern. You are paying the therapist to provide you with the space and support to make it through one of the darkest, hardest times of your life.

Many nontheists have said to me that they either do not go to a therapist or have a hard time fully opening up because of bad experiences with therapists in the past. Many nontheists report having worked with mental health clinicians who have tried to force religious ideologies on them. Worse still, some have reported that they have had therapists tell them directly that the therapist cannot work with them specifically because they are a nontheist. On the one hand, this is wrong and the therapist needs to get some supervision and training if a person's religious belief is the only thing keeping them from working with someone. On the other hand, it is good for a therapist to admit this truth upfront so as to avoid wasting everyone's time and potentially doing harm to the client in the meantime.

Should you decide to see a therapist, it is always your choice as to whether you tell them upfront that you are a nontheist. I get asked quite often what I recommend. I recommend that client's reveal themselves to their therapists in their own time, if at all. Many intake assessments inquire about a person's religious beliefs and most therapists would find it beneficial to know that you are a nontheist upfront. As I have mentioned in other chapters, being that we live in a society where the vast majority of people hold some form of spiritual or religious belief, it is highly likely that your therapist will hold some kind of religious belief or will assume that you do, too. It is also quite possible that a reference to god or faith will slip into the conversation, especially in the context of death. I do recommend that nontheists be mindful of this reality and what is highly likely to happen. That is why, if you choose not to reveal your nonbelief in the beginning, be prepared to reveal it at some point, particularly when you are seeking grief counseling and do not want spirituality brought into the conversation.

I also recommend you have patience with your therapist if you like them. Remember that they are human too and will make mistakes. They will not always say and do everything perfectly. Because therapy can be such an intense process, you can be very vulnerable and therefore get hurt easily. Trust that your therapist does not mean to hurt you. If they do or say something that upsets you, tell them. Do not let it fester to the point that you simply stop returning to therapy. If you like the therapist, you can make the therapist better by offering them your feedback. All businesses want your feedback. A therapist is no different.

Consider Psychotropic Medication

Psychotropic medication is medication specifically for mental and emotional health. When we are stressed, we put a heavy tax on our bodies and can drain them of needed chemicals, hormones, minerals, and vitamins. Some people believe that they can treat a lot of conditions by simply replacing such elements, and so they head to the nutrition shop or health food store to help them during their time of mourning. Ensuring that you have the nutrition you need will go a long way toward maintaining not only good mental health but also good physical health. However, supplements such as multivitamins cannot always meet our body's needs, and we may need to supplement the supplements.

Many antidepressants work as reuptake inhibitors. Our brains are swarming with chemicals. In the world of depression, we most often hear about dopamine, serotonin, and norepinephrine. The most common antidepressants inhibit receptors in the brain from taking in those chemicals. That seems like the opposite of what you would want, right? Actually, you do not want those receptors sucking up all of the good stuff. If they are sucking it all up, that does not leave any for the fluid that surrounds the brain. In the simplest terms, all antidepressants do is prevent those receptors from gobbling everything up so that there is more of it for the brain to use in the appropriate way. Hence, doctors often prescribe selective serotonin reuptake inhibitors (SSRI) and selective norepinephrine reuptake inhibitors (SNRI). Common SSRIs are fluoxetine (Prozac), sertraline (Zoloft), and paroxetine (Paxil). Common SNRIs are duloxetine (Cymbalta) and venlafaxine (Effexor). Medications that impact dopamine are usually reserved for severe depression, schizophrenia, bipolar disorder, and other conditions that might involve psychosis. Examples of medications that affect dopamine levels are chlorpromazine (Thorazine), promethazine (Phenergan), risperidone (Risperdal), and quetiapine (Seroquel).

If a doctor offers you a medication, I suggest that you try to resist the urge to say, *Oh, that medicine is for XYZ disorder! I don't have XYZ!* In my experience as a counselor working closely with psychiatrists who treat my clients, doctors usually do not think of prescribing as "this pill for this diagnosis, that pill for that diagnosis." It is usually more like, "this pill for this cluster of symptoms, that pill for that cluster of symptoms." So even though I just said that certain medications are often used to treat certain illnesses, that is really because certain illnesses typically have certain clusters of symptoms. How is this relevant for the purposes of mourning? Well, if you do not usually struggle with mental health but are struggling with your grieving, you may present with a certain cluster of symptoms that lead the doctor to prescribe any one of a multitude of medications.

The key to successful trials of antidepressants and mood stabilizers is time. Give it time for the medications to work. Unfortunately, many of the medications do have side effects. Most of them are mild, but they are present nonetheless. They usually pass within a few weeks. While people often get upset about the side effects, they often feel even more dismayed if their mood does not improve quickly. However, it can take upwards of six to eight weeks to experience a therapeutic effect of antidepressant and mood-stabilizing medications. Thus, people sometimes give up on their prescription because they suffer negative side effects for several weeks with seemingly no added benefit. I recommend to my clients that they not give up on a trial of medication until they have been on it for at least two to three months, unless, of course, they are experiencing significant negative side effects.

If depression and mood instability are not your problem, another concern might be persistent anxiety. There are classes of fast-acting anti-anxiety medications that do not take weeks or months for you to know how they are going to affect you. Benzodiazepines ("benzos") such as lorazepam (Ativan), clonazepam (Klonipin), and alprazolam (Xanax) will take effect within minutes and last for only a few hours. While these medications are highly effective at treating anxiety, they are also highly addictive and are popular street drugs. As a result, doctors are becoming increasingly hesitant to prescribe them.

In my practice, I have noticed a marked decrease in the use of benzos and an increased use of medications such as hydroxyzine, which is an antihistamine similar to Benadryl. Hydroxyzine, also known as Vistaril and Atarax, is also used to treat anxiety. It is relatively fast-acting, although not quite as fast as benzos, and lasts for hours. What doctors like about it is the low risk of addiction. This medication can be very beneficial as it comes in a range of doses from *take the edge off* to *I need a deep sleep.* Another medication used for anxiety is buspirone (Buspar), which is long-acting, takes time to build up in the system, and is good for problems such as generalized anxiety disorder. This is not for taking the edge off. This is good for those who experience significant anxiety most of the day every day and in almost all situations.

There are many more medications and classes of medications on which I have not touched. The point is, talk to your doctor. Whether you just need a boost to help you get over the hump or you find that your grief is pulling you under water and you are drowning in despair, there is likely something out there that can help you.

Do Not Isolate

When you are grieving, you need to limit the amount of time you spend alone. It is understandable that you want to be alone. You are physically tired. You do not feel like engaging in small talk. Nothing matters now that your loved one is gone. There is nothing that you want to talk about or watch on TV or laugh at. You feel guilty being a Debbie Downer and think that it is a better idea if you just stay away. You want to be free to burst into tears whenever you want to. You are prone to bouts of anger and might lash out at others for doing and saying things you perceive to be insensitive. You decide you would just rather be alone.

I recommend that you find the friend(s) or family member(s) who can and will support you and spend some time with them. It may not be every day or for long periods of time, but even one meal, one TV show, one venting session is better than nothing. You may also find that it is easier to be with one or two people at a time rather than a group of people. People who can be comfortable with being uncomfortable. People who can sit there and let you lie on the couch being sad and listless without being scared away. If you are invited to birthday parties, cookouts, or other social events, it makes sense that it would be hard for you to attend these gatherings, and your friends and family should understand if you have a hard time making them.

However, there must also come a time that you push yourself a little to participate in activities of varying sizes. As I said, perhaps you start out spending time with just one or two people before going to a small gathering or a birthday party. It might be months before you work your way up to attending even small parties. When Tim died, my family reunion was a mere two months later and it was a struggle for me to attend. Part of the way I managed was that I took breaks away from the crowd. On at least two occasions, I walked away from the party just to stroll around the park by myself. One time I even shed a few tears. No matter what, I did not want to miss the opportunity to spend time with family. After all, part of my grief was the overwhelming guilt about not spending more time with Tim. If I had not attended my family reunion and someone in my family died before I got another chance to see them, it would have only compounded my guilt.

Another reason to force yourself to socialize when you are grieving is to fight against the inevitable feelings of guilt about moving on. One moment you will be enjoying yourself with your friends and family and the next you are overcome with the urge to flee the situation so that you can get back to proper mourning. *How dare you abandon your loved one by having fun!* The truth of the matter is that you must have some enjoyment in your life. You must not flee those situations. There will be plenty of time to mourn. In order to have a moment of fun, I started having to remind myself of certain things. Sometimes I even said it out loud: *The sadness is not going anywhere. My loved one is still dead and I am still devastated by it. It is okay for me to have a moment of peace. There is plenty of time for me to be sad and cry.*

Many of us nontheists have already discovered the benefit of a robust online support network and cyberfriends. As tempting as it is to turn off your electronic devices and ignore alerts, try to resist that urge as well. Accept your friends' attempts to support you, even when they are clumsy and sometimes unhelpful. Try to look beyond the words and see the intent. Let their heart emojis and reactions assure you that people care. Now, if their *support* is really just them trying to push religion or other hurtful advice, *It's time for you to move on.* These people not only need to be ignored, but they also need to be put in their place. The beauty of engaging in online activity is that, if they do these things publicly, your tribe will often come to your rescue. But you can also ignore, silence, block, or un-friend them altogether.

During times of grief, romantic relationships may suffer. While many people may find that they have an increased sex drive at various points in their mourning process, perhaps out of a strong need for human connection, it is very com-mon for people to withdraw sexually. You may isolate yourself from your spouse or significant other, or stop dating. Do not be alarmed if you normally have a high sex drive and suddenly you do not. You are exhausted in every way. It stands to reason that you might be too tired for sex quite often as well. If you have a spouse or significant other and find that grief is impact-ing your relationship and your sex life, open communication is critical. In Tip 10, I will address the supporting spouse, but here I am addressing you, the grieving person. Do not with-draw from your significant other. As much as you can, talk openly with them about your loss. They likely want to under-stand what you are going through and want to support you; they just do not know how. If you find that you have a hard time talking to them about sex, grief, or sex and grief, try writ-ing a letter or sending a voice text.

Of course, I am going to recommend counseling. A thera-pist who specializes in relationships may be exactly what you need to facilitate those discussions between you and your significant other. Another thing to consider is that it could be a significant reduction in serotonin, dopamine, or norepinephrine that is reducing your libido, and taking an antidepressant or mood stabilizer might be just what you need to get your love life on track. On the other hand, a known side effect of some medications is a reduced libido. Either way, talk to your doctor!

When you are mourning, you should not be afraid to tell people what it is that you do and do not need. You are going through enough. You are barely hanging on by the sinews of your soul. You need the support of loved ones, but many loved ones do not know how to do that. Many people have not experienced profound loss. If they did, they may not have dealt with it in a healthy manner and, therefore, are not the best guides on how to successfully navigate profound loss themselves. That is why a multipronged approach involving professional and natural supports, prescription and natural remedies, may be necessary if you are to make it through this thing alive and well on the other side.

* * *

Note: If you would like to quickly assess your level of depression or anxiety, there are two common, easy-to-use tools that you can find online. The Patient Health Questionnaire 9 (PHQ-9) and the Generalized Anxiety Disorder 7 (GAD-7) are brief, self-scoring assessments you can take that will give you a sense of whether or not your depression and anxiety levels are high enough that they might warrant professional intervention. Remember, if your scores are very high, it does not automatically mean that something is *wrong* with you. Your level of distress is likely a function of your grief. However, regardless of what the assessment tells you about yourself (i.e., the severity), if the score is high, you should at least talk to your primary care doctor about your symptoms.

Tip 5
There is no time limit on grief. Be patient with yourself.

Every day,
Forever seems further away, yet
Never is always here and
Days toddle by
Nondescriptly

I recall one incident vividly. It involved a woman who I know and love dearly. She is very spiritual and considers herself to be a psychic. It had been a mere three weeks after Tim's death when she responded to one of my Facebook posts that it was "time for me to stop" because my continued mourning was preventing his spirit from "moving on." I responded very angrily that I did not appreciate her response, but it was my Facebook friends, my tribe, that eviscerated her to the point that I had to jump in and reassure them that she was a loved one of mine. Sadly, I have not seen or heard from her since. I hate to think that a relationship has been lost because I was vocal about the fact that I did not like the way she was *supporting* me.

As cliché as it sounds, there really is no time limit to grieving. There cannot be. The pain is too sharp and biting. No one wallows in this kind of misery intentionally. People who suggest that it is time to *just move on* either have never experienced such an intense loss, never fully resolved their grief, or were lucky enough to resolve their grief so quickly that they did not get the chance to develop empathy for those whose grief is not so kind. My aforementioned loved one understood my loss, as she had much earlier lost her husband. However, she had a set of spiritual beliefs to fall back on that we nontheists do not have; she *knows* there is an afterlife. Additionally, her loss was so long ago, she may simply have forgotten the intensity of her grief.

As previously discussed, spiritual beliefs provide a level of support that, for better or worse, have a therapeutic effect that nontheists do not have access to. So, when people suggest that it is time for you to move on, they may also have the experience of depending on prayer, faith, and a belief in an afterlife. If these beliefs provided them comfort, it only makes sense for them to want you to have that same comfort. But they likely do not realize that their access to those tools creates a qualitative difference in how they experience loss. That does not mean that you need to take up prayer to recover from grief. It just means you need to be cognizant of how the presence—or absence—of such beliefs and tools might impact the grieving process.

But what do people mean when they say *move on* anyway?

Do they mean get up out of bed and live your life? Do they mean have another child? Are they suggesting you should re-marry or find another partner? Does it mean put away all of the things that remind you of your loved one? Does it mean stop talking about them? The answer often lies in when they say it, as the timing of the words can reveal a deeper meaning behind them.

For example, if you are in the middle of a conversation about your loved one and someone replies that it is time for you to move on, the message you probably receive is that they are tired of you talking about your loved one. You would probably think the same thing if they responded to a social media post in the same way. It could suggest that they are uncomfortable talking about the person, have no advice for you, or are bored with the conversation. They may not actually be invested in whether or not you move on. However, it definitely feels like they are not invested in you.

If it has been several months and you are working and living life but are not dating, you may have friends and family suggest that you start dating. I think their concern here is not so much about getting over the deceased loved one as it is about doing something that would make you feel good in the here and now. Your friends and family understand that dating, courting, flirting, and having sex are generally good for you physically, mentally, and emotionally. They understand that these activities go a long way toward helping people recover from a depressive episode. What they forget about is that dating, courting, flirting, and engaging in sexual relationships with others can also be fraught with emotional ups and downs. It is not unreasonable for you to want to steer clear of anything that will complicate your emotional health any further.

If your friends and family suggest that you take down pictures and other memorabilia of your loved one, their concern may be that the pictures are what is keeping you stuck in time, preventing you from mentally freeing yourself. Their concern may be that you might have a harder time moving on if your loved one is "watching" you all day. I talk more in Tip 8 about rituals and sacred spaces and ways to commemorate your loved one. While this bit of advice can feel exceptionally cruel, the reason your friends and family could be offering this suggestion makes a tiny bit of sense. I am not suggesting that you should take down pictures and memorabilia. I am merely positing some ideas about why people might say certain things and exploring whether or not there is value in those ideas. Grieving takes time, and you most certainly should not feel compelled to take down pictures if you do not feel that doing so will be beneficial to you.

If it has been six months, a year, or more and your friends and family start telling you to "snap out of it," their real concern might be that you are experiencing a genuine mental health crisis. Consider how it looks to a person who has never experienced this level of grief but sees their friend or family member in such pain. They see crying, loss of interest and appetite, and sleep disturbances. They notice that something about their friend or family member seems to be missing; something about them has changed. All they know is that they want you to be happy again. For some reason, people think that saying, "Snap out of it," will make a person think, *Wow! What have I been doing with myself? Let me snap out of this!* And then actually snap out of it. But of course, we know that is not how it works and, for the life of me, I do not understand why people say that to one another, especially when a person is in genuine distress.

The point is that your friends and family are usually coming from a good place when they tell you to move on, snap out of it, or change some aspect of your life in order to move on. But the truth is that you will never truly move on. You will never be the same. This loss will never be replaced, the hole never filled. You will never completely get over this. But you will have good days again. You will smile again. You will experience happiness again.

When you expect cycles and waves, you can be better prepared for them. You will never be fully prepared for them. Sometimes they will sneak up on you. Other times, you will anticipate their arrival, such as with anniversaries, holidays, and birthdays. However, the intensity of the pain may surprise you. I began feeling the anxiety of the one-year mark of Tim's death two months early. I began noticing that the positive feelings I felt when I thought about him were slowly being replaced by sadness. I was not sure why at first. I eventually remembered that the one-year anniversary was coming up, yet I was surprised that the anxiety was setting in so early.

One month before the one-year anniversary, I began having sporadic crying spells. *Okay,* I thought. *This is to be expected. I can handle this.* I had considered taking the actual day

he died off from work in case I was exceptionally sad but ultimately decided against it. Two to three weeks before the actual
anniversary, I was doing so well that I did not think I would
need an entire day away. Although I was still having the odd
crying spell, I thought I had healed sufficiently and I was feeling good about my progress.

Two days before the anniversary I went to his grave site and
the dams broke free. For over a week afterward, I was positively
inconsolable and I wished I had taken the anniversary off of
work. I lost my appetite again. I became listless. I had to carry
tissues with me everywhere I went in the house. I am lucky
enough to work from home, so I would sign off of work, climb
the stairs, crawl into bed, and stay there until the sun rose and
it was time to do it all over again. I neglected taking my daily
walks. I stopped my daily showers and I even reduced my time
on Facebook and on phone calls with friends and family. Every
tip that I give in this book, I failed to take for myself. Two to
four weeks after the anniversary I was still in quite bad shape.
I was carrying tissues, taking frequent work breaks, and experiencing ongoing bouts of isolation as well as panic attacks.
However, at least I began showering, spending time with family, and hiking again.

I was confounded by how intense, powerful, and consuming the pain was. I dare say I even felt anger toward myself a
few times for having such overwhelming emotions. I was angry at the emotions themselves. I was confused as to how grief
could come back like a best friend I had known my whole life.
But that is exactly what grief is like: a friend—a frienemy—for

life. Grief will be that friend who unexpectedly pops by your house from time to time at inopportune times and disrupts your day-to-day activities. Or sometimes it comes exactly when you are expecting it, but is significantly more unpleasant company than you expected it to be and overstays its welcome. In any case, once grief has found a reason to be in your life, you will never be free of its influence, and only people who have experienced this particular type of loss—the death of a loved one who is part of your soul—can fully understand that.

Persistent Complex Bereavement Disorder

Persistent complex bereavement disorder (PCBD) is an official mental health diagnosis that can be found in the *Diagnostics and Statistical Manual of Mental Health Disorders, 5th Edition* (DSM-5), the diagnostics bible of the mental health world. The DSM-5 recognizes that grief and bereavement must be taken into account when diagnosing major depressive, anxiety, and bipolar disorders. If a person has experienced a recent loss, any mental health professional worth their salt will know to take that into consideration before diagnosing a client with a mental health disorder. However, there are some instances in which we mental health professionals would suggest that bereavement is no longer healthy bereavement, such as when it has taken on pathological qualities.

PCBD is diagnosed only if it has been at least twelve months (or six months in children), since the death of someone with whom the bereaved had a close relationship. That amount of time is important as it goes to the "persistent" part of the diagnosis and takes into account that grief can take a while to move through. But more importantly, the expectation is that, although one might still be grieving at twelve (or six) months, the intensity of the grief has reduced.

A PCBD diagnosis typically involves a "persistent yearning/longing" for the deceased, intense sorrow and frequent crying, a preoccupation with the deceased, and/or a preoccupation with the manner in which the person died. Additional symptoms of PCBD include:

- severe difficulty accepting that the individual has died (e.g., preparing meals for them)

- disbelief that the individual is dead

- distressing memories of the deceased

- anger over the loss

- maladaptive appraisals about oneself in relation to the deceased or the death

- excessive avoidance of reminders of the loss

Individuals suffering with PCBD may also experience suicidal thoughts and urges, feel isolated, be distrustful of others, and believe that life has no meaning or purpose without the deceased. Without the deceased, the individual could lose their sense of identity and feel as if a part of themselves has died or been lost. The bereaved individual might also have difficulty engaging in activities, pursuing relationships, or planning for the future.

One of the most important diagnostic criteria that must be present before making any diagnosis is that the symptoms must cause "clinically significant distress or impairment in psychosocial functioning." The final criterion that must be present to make a PCBD diagnosis is that "the nature and severity of grief must be beyond expected norms for the relevant cultural setting, religious group, or developmental stage." This last criterion is very important because it makes room for the fact that there might be some settings that expect a person to display some—but maybe not all—of these behaviors and, therefore, the clinician must not count those items toward the diagnosis.

Words like "typically," "intense," "frequent," "preoccupied," and "excessive" are vague and subjective terms that reveal why it is important that only trained mental health professionals make diagnoses. When laypeople get their hands on a DSM-5, they often diagnosis themselves and others with fifty disorders. There has been an increase in this phenomenon due to the Internet and the advent of medical sites where we can research symptoms and diseases and convince ourselves that we have some rare disorder—or even that we have only three to six months left to live! Diagnostics is an art, not a science. In other words, do not try to diagnosis yourself just by reading a list of symptoms.

As you can see, there can come a point at which your grief is no longer grief but has turned into a monster that is consuming your life in a scary way. Although there is no time limit on grief, although it comes and goes in waves, although you will have good days and bad, you should also be aware that there are behaviors, actions, thoughts, and feelings that are signs of a much deeper problem and should absolutely be attended to in a clinical setting.

Clinical problems aside, you have to allow yourself as much time to grieve as you need. Significant losses never leave you. It might take a significant amount of time to resolve the intensity to a degree that allows you to live a normal life that is as close to your previous functioning as you can get. Remember in our discussion about how the acceptance stage of grief is a process, not an end point? As Kübler-Ross and Kessler note in *On Grief and Grieving,* "We put the loss into perspective, learning how to remember our loved ones and commemorate the loss." While the acceptance stage might be a process, as a person still grieving as of this writing, I can personally attest to the fact that I sure would love to reach a goal, an end point, at which I could remember my loved one and commemorate the loss without being in so much pain. But here I am, over a year later, still in pain.

Oh boy! This is going to take some time!

Tip 6
Reconnect with nature.

The grief is like water that rushes in to fill a void.
He was so much a part of my soul that nothing is
big enough
strong enough
to fill the void of his absence but grief.

Although the world begins to fade as our minds incessantly work through the five stages of grief, we sometimes find ourselves blankly staring at the world around us. Leaning on the window of a moving car, our head bumping with the road, we try to follow trees that whir by. Melting into pendulating porch swings, we stare at one bird, one squirrel, one bug for minutes on end. Cocooning in oversized sweatshirts under rolling mountains of blankets, we lie on the couch, gaze out the window, and watch clouds until the sky is too dark to perceive them. We may think that we are blind to the world, but typically we are able to take in the natural world while simultaneously living in our internal hell of grief. That is because death is the ultimate reminder of the natural order of things, the circle of life.

The sun rises and sets. Spring and summer bring new life, yet things wither and die in the fall and winter. All living creatures die. Spending time in nature can be very healing as it can remind you that the natural order is beautiful, even when it is dangerous. In fact, some of the most beautiful things in nature are hazardous to you and could bring pain and anguish. Think of views from the tops of massive waterfalls or high mountains! How beautiful they are, yet how painful it would be to fall from such heights. Such is life with love. How beautiful to love someone! Yet we know that, one day, we will all fall in death.

Robert Frost's "After Apple Picking" is one of my favorite poems. On the surface, it is about the speaker's experience one fall day. However, any high school literature student well-versed in metaphors could tell you that the poem is really a contemplation on death.

The speaker clearly has an affinity for nature when he talks of his desire for a "great harvest." One level of meaning is the literal great harvest of his orchard and the other level is a great harvest in his life. The fact that there were "ten thousand thousand fruit to touch" suggests that he had lived a good life. However, the fact that he is "done with apple-picking now" and is "drowsing off" suggests that he is now tired of life. He seems to be aware of the possibility that the tiredness that he feels cannot be resolved by a good long night's sleep. He compares the woodchuck's sleep, which goes into hibernation in late fall, to "just some human sleep." Matter-of-factly and nonchalantly, he indicates that, unlike the sleep from which the woodchuck will awake, humans do not return from this particular type of sleep.

Frost has the reader reflect on life and death through the use of wonderful, sensory-engaging metaphors. It works so well because death is the ultimate reminder of the natural order of things. One way for us grieving nontheists to work through our grief is to embrace that natural order rather than fight against it. While believers and spiritual people turn to their houses of worship, we can turn to the entirety of the great outdoors as our sanctuary. While they have rituals, we can turn to experiences. They have relics; we can have tokens from nature.

Directed Attention Fatigue

In our everyday lives, we slave and toil, rip and run, come and go. We never seem to really turn off. Even when we are able to physically rest, our minds are usually still on, whether intentionally or not. We binge watch TV, work on the weekend, and get on social media for hours at a time. Even when we disconnect from all these activities and get out of the house with friends and family for vacations, stay-cations, or just a night out and about, many of us still regularly post pictures and status updates. Our minds are always on. What is grief but the saddest parts of our mind getting stuck on "on." Statements such as, *we never turn our brains off*, are really referring to something called directed attention.

Attention restoration theory posits that directed attention is a mechanism that, according to environmental psychologist Stephen Kaplan, one of the developers of the theory, "requires effort, plays a central role in achieving focus, is under voluntary control (at least some of the time), is susceptible to fatigue, and controls distraction through the use of inhibition." Directed attention fatigue leads to problems related to our ability to problem solve, control impulses, think clearly, see *the big picture*, plan, follow through with plans, be patient, and so much more. Directed attention fatigue also leads to mood instability such as irritability and anxiety.

In an article for *Journal of Environmental Psychology*, Kaplan suggests that the way to alleviate directed attention fatigue is to engage in "soft fascination." Soft fascination is a form of attention that requires no effort and thus allows us to restore our directed attention, which is perpetually assaulted and engaged in our highly stimulating daily lives. Soft fascination "has a special advantage in terms of providing an opportunity for reflection, which can further enhance the benefits of recovering from directed attention fatigue." Kaplan suggests that nature is a prime "restorative environment" with many opportunities for soft fascination.

Kaplan's research suggests that there are integral components to a restorative environment. First, the restorative environment must involve "being away, at least in principle," because it "frees one from mental activity that requires directed attention support to keep going." Kaplan makes the point that getting away might not always mean a full vacation. It might be as simple as changing what you are looking at. As an avid hiker, I try to find a mountain or trail to get on no less than two Sundays per month. My goal is every Sunday. But for someone who cannot easily manage the four-hour drive it takes me to get to the Smoky Mountains, sitting on a park bench, taking a bike ride around the neighborhood, fishing at a nearby lake, or even sitting on one's own porch might be viable options. The goal is to *feel* mentally free from your daily hassles.

Many researchers are also finding that, if you cannot physically be in nature, looking at images of natural scenes can have positive effects on mood and health. Terry A. Hartig, associate professor of applied psychology at the Institute for Housing and Urban Research at Uppsala University in Sweden, draws on Kaplan's work in his own research. He found that the moods of people who viewed photos of forests were improved versus those who saw pictures of downtown Stockholm. Roger S. Ulrich, co-founding director of the Center for Health Systems and Design at Texas A&M University, produced a well-known study about the effects of window views on surgery patients. As summarized by writer Rebecca A. Clay in an artcile for the American Psychological Association, "He discovered that patients whose hospital rooms overlooked trees had an easier time recovering than those whose rooms overlooked brick walls. Patients able to see nature got out of the hospital faster, had fewer complications and required less pain medication than those forced to stare at a wall." Ulrich also researched heart surgery patients in a Swedish hospital's intensive care unit and found that they, as Clay describes, "could reduce their anxiety and need for pain medication by looking at pictures depicting trees and water."

The second key component of a restorative environment is that it must have "extent." According to Kaplan, "It must, in other words, be rich enough and coherent enough so that it constitutes a whole other world." It must be "a whole other world" because one's mind must be able to fully shift. "It must provide enough to see, experience, and think about so that it takes up a substantial portion of the available room in one's head." It is easy to understand how my weekly romps in the wilderness are "extensive" enough to take up a substantial portion of the available room in my head. The same can be true about the park bench, neighborhood bike ride, local fishing lake, or porch. If you allow your senses to tune in to the natural world around you, in the present moment, and get out of your head, your own backyard can become quite extensive. Let the natural world fill up your mind and displace all of the unpleasant thoughts and emotions with which you have been living in your grief.

The third key component of a restorative environment, notes Kaplam, is that there has to be "compatibility between the environment and one's purposes and inclinations. In other words, the setting must fit what one is trying to do and what one would like to do." Kaplan also points out that compatibility is also related to comfort and demands placed on you. "Thus, in a compatible environment one carries out one's activities smoothly and without struggle. There is no need to second guess or to keep a close eye on one's own behavior. What one does comfortably and naturally is what is appropriate in the setting."

When you are specifically trying to restore is not the time to try something new that would be highly challenging, at least not according to this model. The whole point is to let the thinking, analyzing, problem-solving, hardworking parts of your mind rest. If you are trying to camp in the wilderness but are pitching your first tent and are afraid of nighttime sounds the whole night, you have not rested your mind. If you are afraid of deep water, now is not the time to take up jet skiing. However, if camping or jet skiing are truly your thing and you are able to turn off the hardest working parts of your mind in order to engage in those activities effortlessly, then those might be compatible restorative environments for you.

Start a box vegetable garden. Drink a glass of wine on your deck at night. Take a walk around the neighborhood. Go to that state park you have heard so much about. Buy a pair of binoculars and start birdwatching. (And if you are Black like me, don't let the type of racism that famously occurred in Central Park in May 2020 stop you from trying out this truly engrossing and enthralling activity.) Plant flowers. Sit on the porch—preferably a covered one during a light rain. Take a bike ride. Go fishing.

Do something that gets your physical body out of your house and into the natural world where you can engage all five of your senses. How do you engage *all* five of your senses outside? Sights and sounds are easy, right? Yes and no. Even when I am hiking, sometimes I can still hear traffic off in the distance. In those times, I find something in nature to focus on until that is all I hear and eventually I no longer have to use my directed attention. Usually it is birds or the wind in the trees that I focus on. Sights are easy but you may have to be intentional. After pandemic-related stay-at-home orders were put in place, one of my coworkers commented that she started riding her bike more and realized she had forgotten how beautiful her town is, and she lives in the Tampa Bay area!

It takes even more work to be intentional about smells. I love the smell of a wet forest and mountain laurels. Sometimes I have to literally stop myself in my tracks, close my eyes, and take a deep breath to *catch the scent*. Just like with sounds, once I have noticed that stimulus, I can continuously enjoy it. With feeling, I usually try to find some reason to get my hands in the dirt, rub trees, splash my hands in water. I try to do something that allows my skin to come in contact with the natural world of which I am a part. Taste is the trickiest of them all. Because I clearly cannot go about eating random things found in the woods, I sometimes bring something with me. I know it might sound hippy-ish, but if I think I might want a snack on the trail, I will take something natural like fruit. I am after a fully natural experience, after all. Candy bars, potato chips, and sugary sodas just will not do!

After Tim's death, I did not immediately resume my regular hiking. I just could not drag myself from bed. I did go on a preplanned July Colorado hiking trip, which could not be rescheduled, but once I returned, I went back to ignoring my weekly hiking trips. Eventually I knew I had to restart them. I did it because Tim was proud of me for them. He was in awe of my boldness to wander off into bear country, a Black woman all alone. And he would marvel at my pictures after I posted them online. Every Sunday I could still hear him calling me "Hiker Girl" and I would think, *I've got to get back out there.* When I did finally start going again, I cried a good portion of every hike. Oh, they were such good cries!

When you are grieving, you push your mind and body to their limit and drain them of everything they need to be healthy and cope—hormones, neurochemicals, nutrients, and the like. Your mind and emotions are also under attack as they struggle through the five stages of grief. However, there is clear research about ways that you can rejuvenate, refresh, and restore. I am adamant that reconnecting with the natural world is an essential tool for that healing and recovery process.

Tip 7
Postpone major decisions.

We never got to live.
We only got to love.

Decision-making is best done when your mind is clear and fresh, your emotions stable and in control. When you are grieving, you are in exactly the opposite mental and emotional space. Besides decisions about funeral arrangements, memorials, wills, and estates, etc., I highly recommend that you refrain from making major decisions in the midst of your grief, especially in the earliest days. We can all think of a time or two that we made a poor choice and, in retrospect, chalked it up to having a bad day. There is truth to the suggestion that having a bad day can lead to poor decision-making. What is being in mourning if not a series of the worst days? You probably are not taking the best care of yourself. You may not be well nourished.

Your brain chemicals and hormones may be out of whack. You may be sleep-deprived. Physically, mentally, and emotionally, grief pushes you to the very outer limits of your coping possibilities, and some days you may worry that you might actually fall over the edge. When you are in that much despair, there is no way you should be making major life decisions.

Of course, there are the usual day-to-day decisions that must be made about work, the kids, school, friends, family, and the demands of various other roles and responsibilities. What I am referring to here are major decisions that would change some aspect of your life in a significant and lasting way. For example, you might not want to sell your house (assuming there is no financial pressure to do so) just because you want to get away from certain memories. That pain will subside and you may come to regret your decision to sell the home you shared with your loved one. Taking a new job in another state away from your friends and family might prove to be a disastrous move when you find yourself in need of more than just a pep talk and moral support. The financial strain caused by impulsively buying a new car might haunt you for years if you give in to your desire for some high-end "retail therapy." These are examples of the kinds of major decisions that could potentially be put on hold during our darkest days of grief.

Besides what we know to be true from personal experience—that we often make bad choices when stressed—there is research that bears this out as well. While there is a vast array of research about decision-making in a variety of situations, according to neuroscientists Anthony J. Porcelli and Mauricio R. Delgado, "Research across disciplines supports the idea that [decision-making] processes can be placed on a spectrum ranging from (I) habitual, stimulus-bound, automatic, and less effortful, to (II) goal-directed, flexible, controlled, and more effortful and resource-dependent." In a study regarding how stress impacts decision-making, José Miguel Soares et al. put it slightly differently by saying that decisions are made based on consequences or to increase efficiency. An action based on consequence is "goal-directed behavior [that] is crucial to face the ever-changing environment but demands an effortful control and monitoring of the response." To increase efficiency, "one can automatize recurring decision processes as habits (or rules). Habitual responses no longer need the evaluation of their consequences and can be elicited by particular situations or stimuli."

What does this have to do with making decisions while grieving? This research suggests that, when stressed, the parts of us that are active and deliberate in our decision-making shut down and become less effective. When that happens, we go into autopilot and follow old "rules" or revert to old habits. The process of going back to old habits is not, in and of itself, a bad thing. As Soares et al. suggest, it increases efficiency and reduces stress by reducing the need to put in significant effort or think about the pros and cons of the decision. However, it can become a problem if we get stuck there. As Soares et al. further note, "The ability to shift back and forth between these two types of strategies is necessary for appropriate decision-making in everyday life."

Unfortunately, as Porcelli and Delgado state in a review of the academic literature, chronic stress promotes "an insensitivity to novel goal-directed contingencies." In other words, the decision-making capacities of highly stressed individuals become impaired. Fortunately, research also shows that, because of the brain's renowned plasticity—its ability to bounce back to normal functioning—we can return to our pre-stress, better balanced decision-making processes. "Noticeable, this stress-decision bias was found to be reversible after the end of the stress exposure."

Another reason that it is important to avoid making significant decisions when we are highly stressed is that things that were once rewarding and pleasing to us no longer are. As Porcelli and Delgado point out, "Initial evidence supports the idea that acute stress reduces sensitivity to rewards." Put another way, we need more of the things that we like to make us feel good when we are stressed. If we can normally be satiated with one cookie, during times of stress, it might take four cookies to reach the same level of satisfaction. "Indeed, stress-altered sensitivity to rewarding/punishing . . . appears to play a role in the development of some pathologies including binge eating, pathological gambling, and anhedonia [*the inability to feel pleasure*] in depression." This is why high-end "retail therapy" like buying a new car would be the kind of major life decision that you might need to put on hold during a time like this.

Seek Advice

When you are grieving, you need people that you can turn to

who can help you check your thoughts and decisions. If you have major decisions to make or consider, it might be meaningful to run them by someone first. A trusted friend or family member is a good place to start. Consider an in-law, a school counselor, or maybe even the best friend of your deceased loved one. On the other hand, you must be careful not to be led astray by bad advice or by someone with an agenda at odds with your interests. For example, as a nontheist, friends and family may not always be your best options, especially if they try to push you toward spiritual solutions. You may have to turn to professionals for advice—counselors, bankers, lawyers, health professionals. You must not be afraid to seek help, guidance, and support during these times.

Depending on the reason for seeking the professional advice, I always consider whether talking about my grief would be apropos to the situation. For example, when I had to see a gastroenterologist following Tim's death, I told her about my loss, as I am aware that chronic stress caused by grief can have a negative impact on the GI system. If I were going to the bank just to open another savings account, I probably would not mention it. However, if I were in a situation where my financial situation was negatively impacted by my loss, I would want to discuss that loss openly with my banker, such as I did when I got divorced.

Relationships, Intimacy, and Sex

In regard to making important decisions, how you handle your romantic life during times of grief is very important. I include this specific issue here because the need for love, intimacy, and sex are so innate, you may revert to old habits or make decisions about your romantic life without fully weighing the consequences. My intent here is certainly not to judge anyone. Rather, I simply want to highlight the importance of being exceptionally cautious in this arena of your life when you are grieving.

If you lost a romantic partner, it is easy to initially feel that you should not experience or express any romantic or sexual needs. You may even get the message from others that it is inappropriate to seek to satisfy those needs. However, people can have very different views toward sex. Reasons for engaging in sexual activity can range from simply wanting to relieve stress to wanting to bond with someone we love. Some might also see sex as the very opposite of death in that it is life-affirming—the very act can bring forth new life. According to Kübler-Ross and Kessler,

> When sexual feelings arise after a death, it's easy to judge yourself. How could you have these feelings without your loved one? How *dare* you? It's as if everyone assumes that someone with a loss should never experience normal feelings and desires again. Nevertheless, you do, only this time without your loved one, which seems like a kind of posthumous infidelity. Recognize these feelings as healthy and normal. Do not denounce sex simply because you think you should. Do you denounce food because you always ate with your loved one?

Even if your loss is not that of a romantic partner, grief can drive you to seek solace in the arms of others. And realize, intimacy is not always about sex. Emotional intimacy is just as important as sex and can be just as, if not more so, problematic. I am sure that many can relate to the experience of returning to old flames for support during times of hardship. That is, after all, how I reconnected with Tim. But what if that old relationship was toxic? As the research shows us, habituation drives us to start following old scripts and rules, regardless of how outdated, useless, or harmful those old scripts and rules might be. People talk about following their hearts, but if the executive functioning areas of their brains are failing them, this can cause them to believe their lying eyes and ignore red flags.

You may rapidly find yourself in new relationships during times of grief. Seeking intimacy, support, and the stress relief of sex, you may boldly form attachments to new people despite the tumultuous grieving through which you are going. Remember, you may not be thinking clearly and may not be making the best choices for yourself during this time. Ask yourself why you are in the relationship(s) you are in. Are you genuinely attracted to the person/people, physically, mentally, and emotionally? Are you just using sex to numb your emotions? Do you even care one way or another? How will your sexual choices during this time ultimately impact yourself and others if you are not careful and mindful?

Some cultures have prescribed timeframes in which a person is expected to mourn before they can return to a *normal* life. I would imagine that some people feel ready to return to normal well before their time of mourning is over; others may need more time. What that right amount of time is for you, I cannot say. But beware. As Kübler-Ross and Kessler further note, "Know that the grief will lie in wait until you are ready to deal with it. But we live in the real world, and we do not have grief counselors at our beck and call whenever the pain becomes unbearable. The bottom line is that we are human beings and we do the best we can."

Major decisions are hard to make during the best of times. They are hard to make when you are experiencing normal day-to-day stress. They are exceptionally hard when you are going through what is likely the worst experience of your life—grief. If you have a major decision to make that can be put off for a little while, do so. If something comes up that is not an essential part of your life but has the potential to have a profound impact on it, proceed cautiously. Seek advice and guidance from loved ones or professionals. Recognize that there are real changes going on inside of your brain that are genuinely impairing your ability to make the best decisions at the moment. Pay attention to whether or not you notice yourself falling into old habits, especially unhealthy ones. And take extra special care to guard your heart. Let yourself grieve without the extra pressure of making major decisions.

Tip 8
Do something in their honor.

Rich, warm memories
So vivid in my mind;
Weighty and real.
At times I forget
I'm only remembering.

Part of the incessant ruminating we do when we are grieving is really our attempt at ensuring that we do not forget our deceased loved one. We play movies of them in our minds and spin records of their voice. We place our hands on our cheeks as if it is their hand so we do not forget their touch. We replay sex scenes, sit in their bedroom, play with their toys, call their phones to hear their greetings, replay voice messages they left us, or even eat their favorite foods. By performing mini-rituals such as these, we feel closer to them.

As nontheists, we might not like the word "ritual" because of its close ties with religion. However, common definitions of the word, such as those given by Merriam-Webster.com, include:

- Done in accordance with social customs or normal protocol (such as handshakes or background checks)
- Established form for a ceremony
- An act or series of acts regularly repeated in a set precise manner

Synonyms include *custom, fashion, habit, pattern, practice,* and *second nature.* As you can see, a ritual is certainly more than just a religious activity. Rituals are extremely powerful tools that, when controlled and properly applied—as opposed to letting them control us—can provide the most healing of all of the activities, tips, actions, and recommendations I discuss in this book.

Visit the Gravesite

We nontheists are nothing if not practical. We pride ourselves on our critical thinking and freedom from the drawbacks of supernatural beliefs. Many people think of cemeteries as relics of supernatural beliefs. In many religious traditions, people are buried because they need their bodies—and any possessions with which they might be buried—in order to cross over to the other side or for some form of resurrection. Since most

nontheists do not believe in any kind of afterlife, they have
no qualms about being cremated. Further, many nontheists I
know see no value in cemeteries.

However, there can be something truly comforting about
being able to visit your loved one; it is not nearly as creepy as
some nontheists might think. When Tim first died, I visited
his gravesite weekly, sometimes two or more times per week.
I think I went at least once a week for probably three months.
It became like a drug. It brought me the briefest moments of
relief. Slowly over time those moments of relief would last for
an entire day, then two days, then three. Eventually my visits
became biweekly. Then one weekend I had planned to go after
a hike, but I was extremely tired as the hike had been unexpectedly long and difficult, so I went straight home. The next
few weekends it rained. Before I knew it, I no longer felt the
overpowering urge to visit the cemetery, and it was months before I went again.

I discussed going to Tim's gravesite with a friend of mine
who had lost a lover ten years prior. She is a nontheist and explained that she, too, used to visit her loved one frequently in
the weeks and months immediately following his death. Even
ten years later, she still visits him occasionally. In fact, it is she
who encouraged me to go as much as I needed to, highlighting
how therapeutic it had been for her. As Tim died in June, my
visits, which were sometimes as long as an hour or more, were
during the hottest months of the year. I learned to take something to sit on, water, and plenty of tissues. Luckily Tim's plot
is at the very back of the cemetery with quite a bit of privacy

and shade. I felt comfortable enough to sit there for as long as I wanted, as long as I needed.

One of my editors suggested that the reader might need convincing that visiting the gravesite helps relieve trauma as opposed to creating an unhealthy fixation. Dear reader, I do not have an answer for him. If you are wondering the same, I do not have an answer for you either. I would dare say that anyone who has ever found comfort in visiting a gravesite would say the same thing. In our society graveyards are often portrayed as spooky places whose only value is to scare children. In truth, to someone in deep mourning, they are beautiful places. As the sting of Tim's death lessened, my number of visits lessened. Any fears about what my visits might mean never materialized. It was simple: the gravesite is where my love is and there was where I wanted to be.*

Create a Sacred Space

I know many people who create a sacred space dedicated to their deceased loved one in or around their home. This special place is there to comfort you. Of course, you can also create it with others who might appreciate and benefit from it, for example, the children of the deceased. This special place in your home or yard can be as big or small as you want it to be. It could even be so small that others are not aware of its existence. For example, it might consist of some seashells from a beach trip, small stones that are the loved one's favorite color, or the loved one's favorite plant. To make this special spot a little larger, you could add your loved one's favorite picture of themselves, or maybe the last picture taken of them.

If you want to use real cut flowers, I recommend that eventually you switch to fake flowers. Nothing is more depressing than a vase of dead, moldy cut flowers. You may be able to keep up the fresh cut flowers for quite a while during your heaviest grieving because trading those out is part of a ritual. However, once the ritual loses its necessity, you will begin to forget about the flowers. If the flowers are a key part of the sacred space, though, switching to a high quality set of fake flowers can be an easy solution.

Outdoors, you might find you have a lot more leeway in regard to combining decorations with living plants and flowers, depending on season and space. If you have a house and can plant a garden, you could research the symbolic meanings of plants and flowers and plant ones that are relevant to your situation. Once your plants and flowers are in the ground, you can then add trinkets that amplify nature. For example, wind chimes provide relaxing sounds. I almost always close my eyes and search for the feel of the wind on my face whenever I hear their song. Suncatchers remind us that there is still light in the world, that life is not as grim and dark as our mood feels during our times of grief. You could also put some of your loved one's favorite things in this space. Did they like certain animals? You could get small statues of those animals and place them in the natural area. The most important thing is that the space be meaningful and satisfying to you.

A sacred space or memorial is about reminding you of your loved one. You can do this by putting things in it that are important to you, them, or both of you. Make the special place simple enough so that it does not become a chore to maintain or easily become dilapidated, ugly, or depressing.

Complete a Project

People often have the desire to do something for their loved ones *in memoriam*, but the day-to-day challenges of life, including a lack of available time and resources, may make this difficult. With a little thought, however, you should be able to find a way to honor them in a way that also does some good for you. Perhaps there are activities that you have always wanted to do but never found the needed motivation, such as writing a book, which you could dedicate to your love one. Or maybe there is something that you come across that would be a healthy activity for you, such as training for and running a 5K race that raises money for a cause that your loved one would embrace. Or you might just decide to do some particular thing because it is something that your loved one always wanted to do, such as taking a certain vacation. Whatever it may be, having something to focus your energy and efforts toward, especially when done in the name of your loved one, can be extremely motivating and healing.

I have done two such activities that I dedicated to Tim. In July 2019, one month after Tim's death, I went to Colorado to climb my first fourteen-thousand-foot mountain, a "fourteener" to those who climb regularly. Although this was my second year climbing in the Rockies, it was going to be my first attempt at a fourteener. I had been talking to Tim about it for months.

He had always expressed so much pride in me for taking up hiking, even the hiking I did in North Carolina. But the major hiking I did in Colorado impressed him so! The day I sent him some pictures of a challenging mountain we were considering climbing is the day he started calling me Hiker Girl.* After his death, I decided to dedicate the accomplishment to him. When I reached the top, I went live on Facebook to make the dedication, crying profusely with my hiking buddy, Darrel Ray, who hugged me to help me make it through.*

The second activity I have done in dedication to Tim, as you know, is to write this book. This book was not preplanned. In fact, writing a book about grief had never even crossed my mind. Although I am a therapist who has worked with plenty of grieving clients, and have even given presentations on grief, I had never considered writing this type of book. However, feeling like I was drowning in a resurgence of grief as the one-year anniversary of Tim's death neared, and seeing so many of my nontheist friends struggling with their own grief, one day it just hit me like a ton of bricks: *people need this! I need this!* I emailed my publisher that same day to pitch the idea. By the time I received a positive response the next day, I had already started an outline. I became so motivated and focused on writing that suddenly I was going days, even two weeks at one point, without crying. Almost immediately I could think about Tim and smile again. I could look at his obituary, which sits on my bookshelf in my office, without crying. In the month after I started the outline of this book, I experienced only a few days that were completely lost to overwhelming fits of crying spells. I did have to get through the anniversary of his funeral, Father's Day, and his birthday during that first month, after all.

Although my memorial activities sound big—summiting mountains and publishing books are not easy to do—they are things that I have done before. They felt entirely possible to me. Where you are in your grieving process determines what type of goal you might reasonably set. If you are still grieving so hard that you can barely get out of bed, it may not be realistic to make it your goal to suddenly take up mountain climbing. You want the activity to be something you can start working on immediately, because it needs to be something that will actually motivate you to get out of bed. If you take up an extremely difficult activity, you may not actually find the motivation needed to engage.

If you do not have a lot of energy, a good project might be to create that sacred space inside of the house. If you have a little more energy, you might decide to visit a local place that your loved one always wanted to visit. If you always wanted to run a 5K but are not feeling well, you can start the training process simply by taking daily walks and researching upcoming 5Ks that might be several months away. This will provide a goal that will help get you out of the house and give you plenty of time to train. The key is to assess your level of energy and to be honest about how much you are willing and able to put into the activity. If the activity is too difficult or not really that exciting, you might lose interest, which could in turn increase your grief because of a sense of failure and letting your loved one down.

Throughout life we celebrate and honor one another in a

variety of ways—through parties, awards, gifts, ceremonies, and the like. Although we do these things for the honoree, often honoring others makes us feel just as good. Mirror neurons and dopamine allow us to feel the joy and excitement that the person being honored hopefully feels, and we also feel a sense of connection with others in such celebrations. Therefore, it is not unexpected that we would want to continue this type of activity to honor someone even in death. As nontheists, we realize that our loved one is not looking down (or up!) on us, smiling with appreciation at our efforts. However, we can still feel that same joy that we experience when honoring people who are alive.

Tip 9
Cry. Cry. And then cry some more.

These crying spells are as predictable as high tide and low tide.
Rip currents pull me under
until whitecaps violently heave me ashore,
Abandoned on the hot sands of low tide.
But sure as the wind blows and the moon rises,
High tide pulls me once again into tear-salted waters,
Roiling and boiling with agony and woe above,
A world of wonderment and secret beauty below.

Crying is the most cathartic activity I have ever done. More than a hard run or a hard hike, a hard cry will eventually leave me feeling as physically and emotionally detoxed as any other activity that pushes my body to its limits. Notice I said "eventually," because it is not always the case that I feel so uplifted immediately after crying. Sometimes I do, but not always. Just like with any other activity that places a heavy tax on my body, I require recovery time, and, depending on how hard the activity, my recovery time can vary. For example, hiking to Callow Peak, North Carolina's second highest mountain, via the Daniel Boone trail, an especially nasty and difficult portion of the Appalachian Trail, was hell on my body. I have hiked it twice. And both times my body was angry with me for a week, and it made no bones about letting me know it.

That is how crying can be for me. Sometimes a hard cry is like hiking that stretch of the Appalachian Trail. It might leave me exhausted and spent, but reaching that peak provides a level of catharsis that makes it worth it. Flinging myself down on the stone summit, my body is achy but my mood is lifted. With hard cries, my body and my emotions might remain achy for a little while, but eventually my mood gets a boost. It might be a short-term boost at first, but the longer I grieve and the more I cry, the more of these boosts I experience. These boosts begin to have a cumulative effect, allowing the sadness to fade away as the boosted mood lasts longer and longer.

For some, crying cleanses. In fact, the inhibition of crying due to the belief that crying is embarrassing or a sign of weakness seems to be a modern phenomenon and may be unique to specific cultures. Just look at ancient literature. From the heroes of great epics to stories from the Bible, openly weeping about friends, lovers, family, and even animals was commonplace and even expected. In some parts of the world, it is still common practice and would be considered inappropriate if one were not wailing loudly as one walked through town behind the casket of a loved one. Are these people confused about the healthiest way to grieve or are they on to something?

There is interesting research that supports the belief that crying is beneficial not just on a psychological level but also on a physiological one. What seems to be a consistent finding is that the benefit one perceives to gain from crying is often correlated with their attitude about crying in general. For example, some people believe that crying will decrease stress while others believe it will increase it. Some people worry about whether their crying can be controlled or whether it is even healthy. The research suggests that someone's mental state will influence whether their mood will be lifted after crying. A person's level of introversion and extraversion as well as gender may also play a role here. But much of this is likely mediated by the broader social environment and ingrained cultural expectations. As researchers Asmir Gračanin et al. report,

> the observation that extraverts report more mood improvement may result from the fact that extraverts have more social skills and are better able to elicit social support, that is, to benefit from the inter-individual functions of crying. On the contrary, the fact that men report less mood improvement than women may be connected with the fact that men also report feeling more embarrassed and ashamed than women when crying.

What intrigues me the most, however, are the myriad ways in which researchers are finding that crying is beneficial.

Gračanin et al. provide a summary of existing and emerging research:

- Crying elevates the parasympathetic nervous system (PNS), which is related to relaxation after experiencing periods of intense unpleasant emotion.

- Crying produces oxytocin, "the love hormone," which has well-known stress-relieving effects. Oxytocin and PNS activity are closely related.

- Crying produces nerve-growth factor (NGF) proteins. NGFs are involved in the restoration of neural cells and can be found in tears. There is some evidence that NGFs have antidepressant effects in non-human mammals. Therefore, researchers hypothesize that the mood-enhancing effect of NGFs extend to humans as well.

- Crying releases endogenous opioids into the body. Endogenous opioids are produced during crying episodes and, just like prescription opioids, they relieve pain. Research suggests that they may help alleviate emotional pain as well. More specifically, the researchers predict that, after crying, people experience an increase in emotional pain tolerance.

- Crying impacts the body temperature. Researchers have found that "even subtle increases in cerebral temperature may have impact on the activity of emotion-linked neurotransmitters." Sobbing is "characterized by fast and successive inhalations of air that is, as a rule, colder than body temperature. Thus, according to this hypothesis, sobbing—rather than emotional tearing—might be held responsible for the improvement in mood."

As reported by Sandy Rovner in the *Washington Post*, biochemist William H. Frey's work suggests that tears contain the stress hormones prolactin and adrenocorticotropin. You can see that the notion that crying is good for you is not just something that therapists made up to keep clients coming in the door. It is not something we say just to keep people from feeling embarrassed. The research is beginning to pile up and show that there really is nothing more healing than a good cry.

I believe so wholeheartedly in the power of crying that, if you are the type of person who has a hard time crying, I recommend you try to trigger some tears. Listening to your loved one's favorite songs, looking at pictures, talking to someone with whom you might be comfortable crying—if such a person exists—or, my favorite, going to a secluded place in nature, perhaps with that music and those pictures, might be just what you need. You may need to help yourself get completely relaxed. Much like with an orgasm, if you already have problems getting there, being stressed and tensed will make it all the more difficult to achieve. Help your mind and body relax with things like drinking hot tea or taking a warm bath.

Singer-songwriter Chris Young is the lead singer on the truly touching song "Drowning," in which he and his cowriters, Corey Crowder and Josh Hoge, were all thinking of someone they had lost when they wrote the song. What I like about the song is the recognition that, even though Young might try to resist crying, every now and then he gives in and allows himself a good cry by spending time with old memories.

If you take the mindset that you are preparing yourself for a healing crying session, you can actively prepare yourself for the onslaught of emotions. Steel your heart and mind by relaxing your body. Another analogy would be like getting a tattoo. Those of us who have dozens of tattoos know that it hurts like hell. How do we prepare? By taking deep breaths and relaxing our minds and bodies before getting in the chair. We know the pain is coming. In fact, many of us might even look forward to the pain. We are going to enjoy and revel in it. We just need to prepare ourselves for it first. If you are the type of person who does not cry often or easily, you can do the same knowing that you are going to come out on the other end alive, in one piece, feeling lighter.

It is important to note that research on the benefits of crying frequently discusses the importance of being mindful of whether a person has a diagnosable mood disorder. So even when I say "trigger some tears," please be aware of your overall mental and emotional state. I do not mean to say that you should be moaning and weeping and wailing all the time. Absolutely not! (See my discussion on persistent complex bereavement disorder in Tip 5.) Too much crying *can* be a sign of a bad thing. There can come a point where you need to seek professional support. My intention here is to normalize crying and to encourage those who either cannot seem to cry or who resist crying to give the process a fair shot. At times, we nontheists can get so caught up in being rational that we forget that it's perfectly reasonable to be irrational at times.

With that said, I do want to encourage those who cry regularly to embrace the times when they are not crying. It is easy to feel guilty when you find yourself having even brief moments of enjoyment. Perhaps you feel that you are not entitled to happiness now that your loved one is gone. Maybe you are experiencing survivor's guilt. It could be that you believe you have not mourned long enough. Whatever the reason is, it is not uncommon for us to excuse ourselves from social situations, turn off a good movie, or stop engaging in any kind of pleasurable activity simply because we feel that we do not have the right to be happy. Plain and simple, we feel guilty.

In the deepest, darkest, ugliest times of grieving, you do not have to worry that you will end your period of mourning inappropriately early, if there even is such a thing as "inappropriately early." Even though you might have moments of wavering in this, as a nontheist, you very likely do not believe that your loved one is watching you from the great beyond. So, it is not like they are there judging the extent of your grieving. And you are not competing with friends and family to see who can grieve the hardest and longest. No! You are struggling with an unbearable sadness resulting from the absence of your loved one. In fact, there is research that suggests that we might actually experience real physical pain following the loss of important social connections. As researchers Naomi Eisenberger and Matthew Lieberman note, this is thought to be due to the proximity of the areas of the brain that experience social sadness to those that experience physical pain. Yes! That broken heart of yours really does hurt.

However, you are alive and you must keep living. If you wake up crying, cry while you are getting dressed, cry while driving, cry when music is playing, cry anytime you are alone, cry in the shower, cry in bed, cry at meal time. If you cannot help yourself, then cry, cry, cry. However, it is also absolutely critical that you let yourself experience joy whenever possible. After all, it is not often that you experience pleasant emotions in such a state. Grief subsumes you, overpowers you, and takes control of your life. Its depths are untold. When you are able to break free from its hold and peek your head above water for even ten minutes to breathe the pure air of laughter and smiles, you must take it in as fully as you can, knowing that grief will grab ahold of your feet and legs and pull you under again post-haste.

Tip 10
Caring for others who are grieving.

My heart continues to break, just as I know yours does,
as this past year has gone by at lightning speed.
When people ask me about him, I still have no words.
And I have no words for this card. I just wanted to let
you know that I'm thinking of you and your family,
wishing you strength and peace.

—Card to Tim's mother, 6/8/20

I realize there might be some people reading this book who are not themselves in mourning but rather want to help someone in mourning. However, many natural supports often do not know what to do for their friends and loved ones who are grieving. They feel helpless themselves and, even if they are not grieving the deceased person, they are hurting for their living loved one. This chapter is meant to give those people a few ideas of ways they can help and to reassure them that the things they are doing are helping.

First and foremost, if you are reading this chapter because you want to support a friend or family member, on behalf of that friend or family member, I would like to personally thank you for your love and support. They may not be able to say it right now. They may not even be able to feel the pleasant emotion of appreciation at the moment. They may be too forgetful or exhausted to say thank you. So, for them, I say, thank you. Even if they do not answer the door, respond to your texts, or return your phone calls, they see your efforts and will one day come back to you and let you know how much your love and support meant to them.

With that said, you must try not to let your feelings get hurt when your friend or family member does not respond to your efforts in the way you believe they should. If you have read this entire book, hopefully by now you have a better appreciation for how much anguish they are in and how tough the struggle is. Just as they have to be patient with themselves and just as I implore them to be patient with others, you have to be patient with them. If you recall, Tip 2 is a call for grievers to be patient with others, especially those trying to help them, because those others are probably fumbling in the darkness just as much as they, the grievers, are. So you, the natural support, must guard your feelings closely. When you are hurt, frustrated, or feel slighted, you need to talk about it with someone else. When your friend or loved one is in the deepest parts of their grief, they absolutely cannot handle arguments with others who feel slighted. Do not get me wrong: I am not giving mourners a license to be assholes. I am saying that they literally have diminished energy and coping skills to handle the additional stressors of relationship battles. I could write a whole other book about relationships—romantic or otherwise—during times of grief, but this is not that book. Suffice it to say that if you feel your relationship is terribly damaged during this time, damaged in a way that cannot be momentarily excused or has been excused for too long, then perhaps the two of you can consider getting counseling together. Even best friends can get counseling together. It is not just for couples and biological families.

Expressing Condolences

One way to support your friend or family is to simply express your love and support. By express, I mean verbally and in writing. Genuine forms of expression, both modern and traditional. There is nothing like receiving an unexpected greeting card in the mail. Holidays. Birthdays. Miscellaneous anniversaries. Deaths of loved ones. A card in the mail is such a ray of sunshine to a person's day. I had one friend in particular who mailed me many cards during my first year of mourning. It was the most touching thing. She sent them randomly. She sent them at significant milestones such as three months, six months, and one year. She sent one on his birthday. If I made multiple posts on Facebook about how sad I was, that would trigger her to send one. It overwhelmed me with such bittersweet joy and I would often run to my bathroom to open the card, knowing that I would cry for quite a while upon reading it.*

Knowing how much those cards meant to me, when two friends of mine lost loved ones earlier this year, I mailed them unannounced cards. I received messages that they reacted the same way I had. They had wept intensely, overcome by so many emotions at once. Happy that someone had thought of them. Sad that it reminded them of their loss. Appreciative that the card was nonreligious in nature. Taken aback that someone had spent the time it takes in this day and age to go to a store to buy a real card, go to the post office to purchase a real stamp, use real ink to handwrite a personalized message, and mail a real card—as opposed to doing all of this digitally. A material card and the effort it takes to get it to the person communicates so much more than just the words inside the card.

Pointing out the high value of greeting cards is not to diminish the value of digital forms of communication. Text messages and phone calls can be just as valuable. Of course, today, many people prefer texting to talking on the phone in general. So, know your audience. If your friend or family member did not like talking on the phone before their loss, they likely will not be any more disposed to it now. Times like these are when texts, GIFs, memes, and social media posts come in handy. Although grieving can be such a private process, public social media posts have the benefit of eliciting social support from the larger community. It provides the opportunity for others to chime in with their love and support as well. The post does not even have to be specific. Something as simple as, "Let us show love and support to our friend Candace who is going through a tough time" will trigger others to react and comment, thus showing Candace how many people care about her.

Whatever you do, please, please, please, do not tell them that it is time to move on! Do not question the length of time that they have been mourning. Rather than questioning the amount of time, offer the support we are discussing here. Instead of, "C'mon! It's been six months!" try, "I know it still hurts." Instead of, "Don't you think it's time to move on?" try, "Let's do something new together." The more you validate the person's feelings and reassure them that you are comfortable with their pain, the more comfortable they will be with you. The more comfortable they are, the more receptive they will be to your attempts to help them heal and recover. The more receptive they are, the more they can actually heal and recover.

Spending Time

If your friend or family member will let you in, spending physical time with them is always a good thing to do. Your grieving loved one probably wants to isolate themselves as much as possible. If there is one or two people with whom they can and will spend time, they should. Of course, you cannot, and should not, put your life on hold indefinitely, but your physical presence can be priceless. Even if your friend or loved one sleeps half of the time that you are there, your presence in their home, or them at your home, likely brings about a certain level of relaxation that they may not even be aware of. For example, if it was a spouse who died and they are home alone all the time, having someone else around sometimes might help them feel safe. If they are worried about their own mood because they are extremely depressed, your presence may become the guardrail that keeps them from going over the edge. Sometimes a bestie or buddy being around is better than the flesh and blood relatives in the home.

Over time you can make gentle efforts to get them out of the house or encourage them to engage in pleasurable activities that they once enjoyed. If they once enjoyed eating out but you notice they have not been to a restaurant in months, offer to take them to a new place. You may not want to take them to their favorite place because it will probably remind them of their loved one. As I say all the time, getting in touch with nature should always be on the list of activities. Offer to take them on a scenic drive or to see a waterfall if you are up for a walk. If you live in a city with no car or bucolic scenes, find the nicest park you can access via public transportation and go for a picnic. Most medium-to-large cities have botanical gardens that are free to visit and are perfect spots for lunch.

Providing Relief

Just because someone dies does not mean the world stops spinning. Our lives must go on, and go on they do. Your grieving friend or family member likely feels like the world has sped up to lightning speed just at a time that their fuel is running low. Unfortunately, jobs nowadays only offer a few bereavement days, even for deceased spouses and children. Without available sick or vacation days, or unpaid time off, people might have to go back to work even before the funeral! Schools can allow only so many excused and unexcused absences before students are failed or held back or courts are involved. Land-lords and utility companies offer no grace periods due to death. Therefore, your grieving friend or family member can easily become overwhelmed by day-to-day responsibilities as they are forced to *get back to normal* at a time when their world is the most abnormal it has ever been.

You can provide relief in a variety of ways. For example, one of the most common ways that people offer their services to those in mourning is by cooking. Providing food for those in mourning can literally be a lifesaver. As discussed earlier, those in mourning will easily neglect their physical needs, in-cluding the most basic need for food and water. It may be that they simply do not perceive hunger or it could be that their energy level to cook or even walk to the kitchen is so low that hunger is of no consequence. Having delicious and enticing foods already prepared can sometimes be just the thing some-one needs in order to get them to eat. I might not be motivated to eat a bowl of cereal or a microwaved frozen meal, but you might win me over with homemade macaroni and cheese and fried fish with hot sauce!

But, beware. There is a drawback to all of the homecooked meals. Leftovers and dirty dishes! If every other day someone is dropping off a casserole, what is a person to do with all of the casserole dishes? If you are going to be delivering food, consider dividing it into small portions and using disposable pans, bowls, and dishes. One of my friends brought me a quart of some of the most delicious homemade soup. I am embar-rassed to admit that I could not manage to eat the entire quart, and more than half of it ended up molding in the refrigerator before I threw the disposable container into the garbage. Your friend or loved one may similarly end up feeling bad about wasting your food, too. But do take food. Just try to take modest portions based on how many people are in the home and be sure to use disposable containers.

Also, I know I just said that I would prefer homecooked soul food over mass-produced, prepackaged foods, but those foods do have their place. Consider buying foods that come in individually wrapped portions and have longer shelf lives. For example, peanut butter crackers became my best friend for months because they did not upset my stomach. I bought a box of them that had several of the six-cracker packs. Sometimes those six crackers would last me two or three days. Along with water and maybe some plain tuna, that would be about all that I could eat. Canned tuna is a good idea because of the small portions and the high protein. If you buy cereal and milk, consider getting a quart of milk. Smaller portions, remember.

If you are feeling especially generous, assisting with household chores might offer some necessary relief to those grieving. Survey your friend or family member's home. If dishes need doing, do them. Do not ask, "Do you want me to do your dishes?" They are probably going to be too embarrassed to say yes. Just do the dishes. Help pick up the house. Wash a load of towels. Or, if it is within your means, offer to pay a cleaning service to give the entire house a deep clean. We all know how good it feels to come home to a fresh, clean home. It can do wonders for lifting a mood. In order to offer this kind of help, you might have to broach the topic very gently. People are often embarrassed by dirty or messy homes. If you offer to pay a professional to clean their home, they may interpret that as your suggesting that their home is so filthy that only a professional can handle it. You may want to preface the offer by explaining that you realize how stressed they are and that you simply want to help them have a fresh start as they begin rebuilding a new normal.

Another significant bit of relief you can provide is child-care. Whether they need assistance with childcare for work or they just need a day off, not having to worry about the safety and well-being of their child for a while is priceless. The need for a break from infants and toddlers is the most apparent, but even elementary and middle school–aged kids require a degree of energy that might be difficult for a person in mourning to muster. They need meals cooked, help with homework, people to chat with about school, chauffeurs, and so much more. Grieving parents need help with all of these things. I feel incredibly lucky that I have only one child and she was a rising junior in high school at the time of Tim's death. But she was in the sixth grade when her father became ill and I do not know how I would have made it without my extensive support network. I had so many friends and family whom I could call on at the drop of a hat for childcare, emotional support, and material support. I think I literally would have had a nervous breakdown had it not been for them, Tim included.

Touching

There is nothing like a long, firm bear hug. Do not be shy but know your audience and whether or not they like to be touched, and never touch without first obtaining consent. Do not even touch a child until you have asked if it is okay to give them a hug, a "squeezie," a pat on the back, or a flight like Superman across the room. Consent. Consent. Consent! Human touch is essential to healthy growth and development. It is well documented that babies who do not get much human contact after birth develop a variety of physical and emotional health complications as they grow up. Human touch produces oxytocin, the feel-good hormone that promotes human connection and decreases distressing emotions such as depression and anxiety. Oxytocin is also why so many people develop emotional attachments to their sexual partners, even when they are determined not to. Our bodies produce oxytocin when we hug as well. When in doubt, when words fail you, offer a hug—a deep, meaningful embrace that communicates that you are truly there for that person.

In the introduction, I talked about how one of my good friends hugged me and let me cry on her lap outside of the church during Tim's funeral. A strong hug helps a mourning person feel like someone is holding the pieces of their body together at the moment that it feels as though they might crumble into a thousand parts. A warm hug reminds a grieving person that they are alive as they listen to the other person's heartbeat. A hug that does not shy away even when the mourner might be secreting tears and mucus down the hugger's nice, black dress communicates unwavering care, concern, and support.*

Sex Life

The sex lives of spouses and significant others can often suffer during times of grief. As I noted in Tip 4 on attending to your psychological and emotional needs, grieving people tend to isolate and that can extend to their romantic relationships as well. A mismatch in libido between the grieving person and their partner(s) can be a recipe for disaster, especially if the period of grief is profound and extended. The key to surviving this time is communication. You may consider seeing a relationship counselor to talk through not only the sexual issue but also any other issues that are likely bubbling just below the surface.

As the support, you must be patient. It could be that your partner would like to have sex but just needs more time to get in the mood than they used to. You know your partner. Do the things that they love. Speak to them in their love language. What lifts their mood? What makes them happy? What puts them in the mood? What makes them feel sensual? Try talking openly about it. Many couples do not talk openly about their sexual wants, needs, and desires. Now may be the time to do that. If it is uncomfortable, you may try writing letters to one another.

The most important piece of advice that I have for you, however, is that you do not engage in guilt-tripping, gaslighting, shaming, or forcing your partner into sexual activity of any kind. Period. How do I define that? Did your partner state, "No"? If they did, then you must stop. Period. Did your partner seem unsure, shy away, push you away, pull away from you, walk away, or do anything that left you wondering if they really wanted you? If you are unsure, then you must stop. Period. If your partner does not want to engage in intercourse, requesting some alternate activity such as a hand job or oral sex is inappropriate. Period.

What is acceptable is for you to get comfortable with masturbation. Let us just be honest. Your partner is going through a hard time and so are you. It can be difficult to support the person you love in their time of bereavement. It is not easy to watch them be in such pain day in and day out. You need stress relief as well. If your grieving partner is not able to satisfy you in the way you want, you may literally have to take your pleasure into your own hands in order to obtain your own stress relief. And that is okay. But if that is still not enough and the relationship is becoming strained, you should start searching for a couple's counselor.

Grief is hard both for the one in mourning and for those trying to support them. You might get exhausted, too. You might feel hopeless and helpless seeing your loved one in so much pain. Accepting that there is nothing you can do about it and that they just have to go through a unique, individualized process allows you to focus your efforts on concrete, helpful actions that require little to no input from them. You become the most supportive when you position yourself in the outskirts of their world, unimposing but visible and present.

A Caveat of Pandemic Proportion

As 2020 taught us, spending physical time with your friends and family may not always be possible, at least not in close quarters. But even when that's the case, technology now allows novel ways for us to see one another, such as through video calls. You can even watch a movie simultaneously, such as through social media sites and apps. Tech companies are creating all sorts of fun ways to increase our interactions and to improve our ability to socialize when opportunities for in-person activities are restricted or limited.

Similarly, cooking, cleaning, or bringing food to a friend or loved one may not always be possible, but you can always hire a professional cleaner for them or have food delivered to their door. You can even send groceries, over-the-counter medicine, and just about anything else you can think of through apps and online sites. With the internet and e-commerce, there are literally thousands of ways to get food, goods, and services to our friends and loved ones when we are unable to be in their presence. The point is, do not give up on supporting your loved one in tangible and material ways, whether there's a pandemic that requires social distancing or whether you live on the other side of the country or globe.

Conclusion

"The will to save a life is not the power to stop a death."
—Elisabeth Kübler-Ross

You can make it.
This is your new normal.
It will get better.
You will make it through this.

You will survive.
You must survive.

This is your new normal.

References

Rebecca A. Clay, "Green Is Good for You," *APA Monitor* 32, no. 4 (April 2001): 40, www.apa.org/monitor/apr01/green-good.

Naomi I. Eisenberger and Matthew D. Lieberman, "Why Rejection Hurts: A Common Neural Alarm System for Physical and Social Pain," *Trends in Cognitive Sciences* 8, no. 7 (2004): 294–300.

Asmir Gračanin et al., "Is Crying a Self-Soothing Behavior?" *Frontiers in Psychology* 5 (2014), www.frontiersin.org/articles/10.3389/fpsyg.2014.00502/full.

Stephen Kaplan, "The Restorative Benefits of Nature: Toward an Integrative Framework," *Journal of Environmental Psychology* 15 (1995): 169–182.

Elisabeth Kübler-Ross and Davis Kessler, *On Grief and Grieving: Finding the Meaning of Grief Through the Five Stages of Loss* (New York: Scribner, 2005).

Anthony J. Porcelli and Mauricio R. Delgado, "Stress and Decision Making: Effects on Valuation, Learning, and Risk-Taking," *Current Opinion in Behavioral Sciences* 14 (April 2017): 33–39, www.ncbi.nlm.nih.gov/pmc/articles/PMC5201132/.

Sandy Rovner, "The Chemistry of Crying," *Washington Post*, October 6, 1987, www.washingtonpost.com/archive/lifestyle/wellness/1987/10/06/the-chemistry-of-crying/46e8973b-9bc9-43b6-905b-07c65beef630/.

José Miguel Soares et al., "Stress-Induced Changes in Human Decision-Making Are Reversible," *Translational Psychiatry* 2 (July 2012).

About the Author

Candace R. M. Gorham, LCMHCS, a licensed mental health counselor, is a former ordained minister turned atheist activist, researcher, and writer on issues related to religion, secular social justice, and the African-American community. Having worked as a mental health counselor for more than ten years, her primary focus is on at-risk youth and family therapy, with an emphasis on depression, anxiety, and mood disorders. She is the author of *The Ebony Exodus Project* and a member of the Black Humanist Alliance of the American Humanist Association, the Secular Therapist Project, the Clergy Project, and the Secular Student Alliance Speaker's Bureau. Candace resides in Greensboro, North Carolina, with her teenage daughter.